Coasters of South Wales

by

Bernard McCall

INTRODUCTION

This volume looks at ports between Swansea in the west and Chepstow in the east. The industrial revolution saw a huge and rapid expansion of ports in this area, thanks largely to the insatiable appetite for coal and metals which could be supplied in abundance from South Wales. The latter half of the twentieth century saw an inexorable decline in the area's coal production and heavy industry with the inevitable result that large sections of port areas have declined in maritime importance. The last two decades have seen many of these dockland areas being redeveloped for commercial, residential and leisure uses. Many of the photographs have been selected because they illustrate the changing scene in traditional port areas. I have never been enamoured of the school of ship photography which claims that the best photograph is the three-quarter bow shot of a vessel at sea or without background. The purpose of this series of books has been to put the featured ships in a geographical and historical context. This volume, perhaps even more than previous volumes, illustrates the importance of such an approach.

Furthermore, I have taken this opportunity to include as many views as possible of unfamiliar wharves and jetties, especially those on the River Neath and River Usk which have been very much neglected by photographers over the years. The desire to include as much material as possible in order to illustrate the many relatively recent changes in port landscapes has meant that this is the first book in this series to have 96 pages instead of the usual 80.

A worrying issue that has arisen during research for the captions in the book is that many changes have gone unnoticed or unrecorded. Equally worrying is the fact the some recent changes have been carelessly or incorrectly recorded. As one example, reputable websites quote the date of closure of the Llandarcy oil refinery variously as 1997, 1998 or 1999. That three dates are given for an event that happened within the last fifteen years is astonishing.

For readers unfamiliar with maritime books such as this one, perhaps I should explain the information given in brackets after each ship's name. The three letters are an abbreviation of the national flag flown by the ship - details are on page 96. The next figure is followed by grt (gross registered tonnage) or gt (gross tonnage). Space precludes a detailed explanation of these figures and the difference between them. Suffice it to say that both are a measurement of the internal volume of a ship (not its weight). New measurement rules were adopted from 1994 so vessels photographed prior to that date will generally have a grt figure and after that date they will generally have a gt figure but much depends on the date that changes from grt to gt were recorded. I hope that general readers will not be deterred by the provision of this information. The final two digits indicate the year in which the ship was completed.

Acknowledgements

As always, I must thank the photographers who have so willingly made available to me their valuable images and also passed on a huge amount of local knowledge. It has often been difficult to select an image from the many that were loaned to me. I would also like to thank the local staff of Associated British Ports and Briton Ferry Shipping Services for information about their port areas. I am especially grateful to those individuals who provided detailed information about wharves on the River Usk, the maritime history of which has been sadly neglected. Thanks go to my two main proof readers, Gil Mayes and Iain McCall, who have eliminated many errors. Every effort has been made to check all information in the captions. I apologise in advance for any errors that may exist and I claim sole credit for such errors. As always, I thank the staff of the Amadeus Press for their work in the production of the finished book.

Bernard McCall   Portishead   September 2011

Published by Bernard McCall, 400 Nore Road, Portishead, Bristol, BS20 8EZ, England.
Telephone/fax : 01275 846178.   E-mail : bernard@coastalshipping.co.uk   Website : www.coastalshipping.co.uk
All distribution enquiries should be addressed to the publisher.

Printed by Amadeus Press, Ezra House, West 26 Business Park, Cleckheaton, West Yorkshire, BD19 4TQ.
Telephone : 01274 863210.   Fax : 01274 863211.   E-mail : info@amadeuspress.co.uk   Website : www.amadeuspress.co.uk

ISBN : 978-1-902953-56-4

Front cover : Many shipowners are synonymous with the coal trade, perhaps none more so than William Cory & Son Ltd whose funnel colours of a black diamond on white band on black funnel symbolised that trade. The **Corbrae** (GBR, 2002grt/52) was built by the Burntisland Shipbuilding Company and was launched on 25 June 1952, being handed over on 18 September. In July 1971, she was bought by Stephenson Clarke and remained in the coal trade as **Brightling** but this proved to be brief. She was sold to Cypriot flag operators in 1973 and was renamed **Kappa Junior** although that same year saw her renamed **Arbnama** and then **Verza** in quick succession. Before further name changes could be made, she was wrecked on 27 March 1974 during a voyage from Casablanca to Granville with a cargo of phosphates. The photograph was taken at No. 13 coal hoist in Kings Dock, Swansea, on 27 May 1970.
(John Wiltshire)

Back cover : Hopefully, readers will appreciate the references to industrial history and archaeology within the pages of this book. Both merge splendidly with the landscape in this photograph of Giants Wharf on the River Neath on the evening of 20 May 2001. The **Vistafjord** (MLT, 1437gt/67), built at the J J Sietas shipyard near Hamburg, loads aluminium salt slag for Raudsand in Norway whilst the Elsfleth-built **Vera** (ATG, 2958gt/80) discharges coking coal from Antwerp. In the distance to the far left can be seen Neath Abbey Wharf at which a veteran lightship is moored, and just beyond is a bridge taking a freight railway line over the river. This is claimed to be the only skew swing railway bridge in the country although its days of opening to allow the passage of vessels to the town wharf in Neath are long gone.
(Bill Moore)

The **Whitsea** (GBR, 728gt/71) manoeuvres alongside the **Super Ferry** (MLT, 14797gt/72) to deliver bunkers on the evening of 1 August 1999. During the period of peak summer sailings, the bunkering of the Swansea - Cork ferry had to be a quick operation as the ferry was generally alongside for only two hours. The bunkering tanker would usually be waiting in Swansea Bay and would follow the ferry closely up the channel in order to secure alongside within a few minutes of the **Super Ferry** being made fast at the ferry port. The **Whitsea** was one of several small tankers built to dimensions that would allow her to deliver oil products to Quedgeley on the outskirts of Gloucester. She was launched by Appledore Shipbuilders on 18 September 1971 and delivered as **Bude** on 5 October to owners Bowker & King. She continued to trade mainly in the Bristol Channel after the closure of the Quedgeley oil depot in 1985 and was eventually sold in May 1992 to John H Whitaker (Tankers) Ltd by whom she was renamed **Whitsea**. In March 2008, she was acquired by owners in Lagos, Nigeria, and was renamed **J. Blessing** under the flag of Honduras.

(Bill Moore)

On page 13, we refer to the Dragon Line service conveying containerised coal from Swansea to Belfast. For much of its duration, this service was operated by the **Kenmare** (ATG, 2435gt/68) seen from the eastern breakwater as she arrived at Swansea on 15 October 1994. She was one of two sisterships built at the Schlichting Werft shipyard in Travemünde and which entered service on the Irish Sea but working from Preston. Originally named **Marietta Bolten**, she became **Hermia** in 1974 and **Kantone** then **Kenmare** in 1987. As such she loaded containerised coal initially at Garston for delivery to Belfast and transferred to Swansea after the departure of the **Brynmore** in late 1988.

On 12 December 1995, she made contact with the **Worthing** (GBR, 1938gt/75) when leaving Belfast but damage was only slight. In mid-July 1997, she was laid-up in Swansea and was subsequently detained before being sold a year later. Leaving Swansea on 12 September, she then loaded at Felixstowe and Harwich before departing to the Persian Gulf via Malaga, Limassol and Port Sudan. At some stage on this voyage, she was renamed **Ahmad B** under the Cambodian flag. It was reported that she reverted to **Kenmare** in 2004 before becoming **Sara** in 2005, since when there has been no information about her.

(Nigel Jones)

The Charles Connell shipyard at Scotstoun on the River Clyde was well-known for the construction of cargo liners. The Connell family happened to be close friends and neighbours of the Struthers family which owned the long-established shipping company of J & A Gardner & Co Ltd so it was no surprise when the latter asked the shipyard to build a coaster to replace its *Saint Kilda* (GBR, 708grt/55) which had sunk off Caldy Island on 25 November 1961. With the Connell yard having no other orders at the time, the *Saint Aidan* (GBR, 973grt/62) was built quickly and was virtually complete when launched on 26 March 1962. She was handed over after successful trials on 9 April. She remained in the fleet for twenty years until sold to owners in the West Indies to whom she was handed over on 27 May 1982. She retained the same name until 1985 when a further sale saw her renamed *San Andres*. She remained listed in *Lloyd's Register* until 2010 but her fate is unknown. The *Saint Aidan* was one of three ships in the hard-working Gardner fleet most frequently used for coal cargoes and she was awaiting entry to Swansea when photographed on 12 June 1971.

(John Wiltshire)

On a sunny day, late afternoon and evening always offered excellent lighting for any photographer who was standing on Swansea's western breakwater or approach to it. These were ideal vantage points for ships entering or leaving the lock. On 17 June 2004, the **Fast Ann** (VUT, 1740gt/80) is outward bound with a cargo of steel coils for northern Spain. She is one of four examples of the Type 104a design from the J J Sietas shipyard at Neuenfelde on the outskirts of Hamburg. We shall see another example on page 26. We shall also see three more examples of Fast Lines vessels. The **Fast Ann** was delivered to German owners as **Saphir** on 23 March 1980. She became **Fast Ann** in 1992. Two drydocks were built at the western end of Kings Dock. The first of these was Palmers Drydock, built in 1924, and adjacent to it, the much larger Duke of Edinburgh Drydock was built in 1959. Both fell into disuse and it was a pleasant surprise when it was announced that the larger dock was to be reopened and refurbished in 2009 after the winning of a contract to overhaul the cruise liner **Saga Pearl II**.

(Bill Moore)

The first two enclosed docks in Swansea were the North Dock and South Dock, situated on the west bank of the River Tawe. North Dock closed in 1930 and South Dock closed in 1971 but has been reborn as the city's Maritime Quarter. By 1870, Swansea was handling over 1.5 million tons of cargo annually. Nine years later, construction began of the first enclosed dock on the east of the Tawe. This was Prince of Wales Dock, completed in 1881 and extended in 1898. Although the dock has become the centre of the SA1 redevelopment scheme, cargoes of sand are still brought in. The dock has also been used to lay up vessels. Such was the status of the **Lancing** (GBR, 1765grt/58) when photographed on 4 March 1970. A product of the Austin & Pickersgill shipyard in Sunderland, she was launched on 5 December 1957 and delivered to Stephenson Clarke in March 1958. She was lengthened by 6,1 metres in 1969 and was sold in 1978. Her new owners must have been lacking in imagination (or paint) when they renamed her **Landing**. After a further ten years, she was sold to Greek owners and renamed **Galini**. As such she was still listed in *Lloyd's Register* in 2010 although a report from Greece noted her demolition in 1995.

(John Wiltshire)

This photograph is dated 30 July 1994 and also arriving for laying up is the coastal tanker **Breaksea** (GBR, 992gt/85). She is approaching Tennant's Wharf in the Prince of Wales Dock at the end of a voyage from Dublin. Six days previously, there had been a major explosion and fire at Texaco's oil refinery on Milford Haven after it had been struck by lightning. Production was halted and the **Breaksea** was sent to Swansea for short-term lay up until production resumed or an alternative charter could be arranged. In the event, she was trading again within a few days. The tanker was built at the Nordsøværftet shipyard in Ringkøbing. She was launched on 10 May 1985 and delivered to Bowker & King Ltd on 18 July. The company was subsequently taken over by Crescent Shipping which was itself in turn taken over by other interests. The **Breaksea** herself was sold to Nigerian owners and left the British coast for Nigeria in late 2005. The Prince of Wales Dock had, of course, been used for exporting coal. The dock's last coal hoists were scrapped in 1966.

(Bill Moore)

In 1918, the first oil refinery to be built in the UK was completed on the outskirts of Swansea. This was the Llandarcy refinery, built by the Anglo-Persian Oil Co, later to become British Petroleum. Two years later, Queens Dock was opened to serve the refinery. This dock utilised a large expanse of water that had been enclosed during the construction of a long breakwater to protect Kings Dock. The closure of the Llandarcy refinery in 1998 and the later closure of the BP Chemicals plant at Baglan Bay (see page 26) in 2004 have meant that Queens Dock is now redundant and no doubt destined for redevelopment. Photographs of coastal vessels in Queens Dock are surprisingly rare. The **Lilleborg** (DNK, 299grt/61), seen on 19 February 1971, was built at the Nobiskrug shipyard in Rendsburg for a consortium of Danish owners. She was launched on 26 October 1961 and handed over after successful trials on 20 December. She retained her original name of **A.N.P.** until being sold to Ebbe Wedell-Wedellsborg, a member of the original consortium, and taking the name **Lilleborg** within his Dannebrog fleet. On 30 March 1971, she was sold to Hans Petersen, of Årøsund, and was renamed **Inger Lupe**. Two years later, she began a charter in the Persian Gulf and never returned. Her owner, however, was declared bankrupt in 1985 and the tanker was soon sold to owners in Abu Dhabi by whom she was renamed **Al-Markhaniya**. She is thought to be still in service under this name.

(John Wiltshire)

The **Lincoln Ellsworth** (NOR, 1066grt/66) was named after an American explorer. The liquefied petroleum gas tanker was built at the A. G. Weser Seebeck shipyard in Bremerhaven. She was launched on 17 December 1965 and handed over to Oslo-based Einar Bakkevig in September of the following year. In late August 1981, she was laid up at Sandefjord in Norway and in 2003 was sold to Copesul-Companhia Petroquimica do Sul in Brazil. Named **Tacosul** under the Panamanian flag, she left Sandefjord on 19 March 1983 and arrived in Rio Grande on 15 April. She then entered service between the latter port and Porto Alegre. In 1990 she was sold to Copesul-Companhia Petroquimica do Sul and bareboat chartered to Navegação Guarita for the carriage of cargoes such as propene, ethene and butadiene. Since then she has been sold twice within Brazil and in 2011 her cargo tanks were removed so that the nickel content could be otherwise used. At the time of writing, the hull remains in Porto Alegre with an uncertain future. We see her in Queens Dock on 5 September 1972.

(John Wiltshire)

We now move to Swansea's Kings Dock to see a classic collier of one style in a classic setting. Construction of Kings Dock began in 1904 and it was formally opened five years later. On 5 November 1973 the **Worthing** (GBR, 1873grt/57) is waiting to load at No. 15 hoist. She was launched at the Hall, Russell shipyard in Aberdeen on 24 June 1957 and delivered as **Dulwich** to the South Eastern Gas Board in October of that year. She is a good example of what was known as the "flat-iron" design for delivering coal to gas works and power stations upriver on the River Thames which required navigation beneath low bridges. In 1970 she was acquired by Stephenson Clarke and was renamed **Worthing**. Seven years later, she became **Worthy** when bought by Cypriot-flag operators. A further sale in 1980 saw her renamed **Antigone P** (rendered as **Antigoni P** in some sources). On Christmas Day 1981, she arrived at the Catalonian port of Villanueva y Geltru (Vilanova i la Geltrú) for demolition. The coal hoist was demolished, along with No. 14 hoist, in 1984.

(John Wiltshire)

Our next three photographs take us ever further back in time to look at former British colliers still being used to load coal in Kings Dock after leaving the Red Ensign. The newest of the trio is the **Sageorge** (CYP, 1837gt/53). She was also in the Stephenson Clarke fleet; in fact she was built for this company at the S P Austin shipyard in Sunderland where she was launched on 4 November 1952 with completion coming in February 1953. She was named **Hayling**, following her owner's tradition of naming vessels after towns and villages in Sussex and Hampshire. She was sold to Cypriot-flag operators and renamed **Sageorge** in 1970 and is seen at No. 12 hoist on 22 February 1971. She was wrecked on 29 April 1972 after grounding on the coast of south-eastern Crete while on passage from Ashdod to Genoa with a cargo of phosphates.

(John Wiltshire)

It could seem that a vessel the size of the **Carmelina** (PAN, 3105grt/46) is possibly too large for inclusion in a book about coasters but she has an impeccable coasting history. A gearless collier, she was built for the Hudson Steamship Co Ltd by the Ailsa shipyard in Troon. She was launched on 27 June 1946 and handed over as **Hudson Strait** in October. In December of that year, she loaded 800 tons of open cast coal at Blyth, the first such export from that port. The fact that she had five holds rather than the more usual four meant that she could carry more grades of coal. She was the first of three Hudson colliers to be sold for further service under the Panamanian flag in 1966/67. Italian operators paid £25,200 for her and she was handed over at Denton Tier on the Thames on 5 January 1967. We see her as she loaded coal, again at No. 12 hoist, on 24 August 1969. In late 1975, she was sold to shipbreakers at Vado Ligure.

(Bob Allen)

The **Costicos** (LBN, 2993grt/39) is the oldest of the trio and again is seen at No. 12 hoist. The date was 20 August 1969 and she was yet another classic collier built for British owners at a British shipyard. She too was a product of the S P Austin & Son shipyard and was launched as **Lea Grange** at this company's Wear Dock yard on 12 October 1939. She was delivered two months later to the Tanfield Steamship Company, of Newcastle. Sadly, there seems to be no information about her work during World War 2 although it would be safe to assume that she carried coal from the north-east of England to the south. She was acquired by Stephenson Clarke in 1953 without change of name and six years later was sold to Lebanese flag operators by whom she was renamed **Costicos**. She served them for twenty years until towed to Istanbul for demolition in June 1973.

(John Wiltshire)

In 1913, there were 26 coal hoists in Swansea's various docks, all of course served by rail and operated by hydraulic pressure. The last two hoists to be demolished were No. 12 and No. 13, the last loading from a hoist being on 25 February 1987. Our final view of traditional coal loading in Kings Dock shows the **Saga** (GRC, 2573gt/51) on 21 October 1970 with a wagonload of coal being tipped from No. 13 hoist into the ship's forward hold. The ship was launched at Kristiansand on 24 April 1951 and delivered to local owners as **Aquila** during July. Sold within Norway in 1964, she was renamed **Joquila** and became **Saga** three years later when bought by German owners. Surprisingly, she was not renamed when bought by Greek owners in 1969. She suffered a fire in her hold when berthed at Hull on 3 September 1972 and eventually arrived for demolition at Bilbao on 25 July 1973.

(John Wiltshire)

In 1987, a new service was established shipping containerised coal from Swansea to Belfast. It was estimated that 150,000 tons of coal would be thus exported annually from the Welsh port to Belfast. For the service, the **Brynmore** (DEU, 3120gt/84) was chartered by Dragon Line, a subsidiary of the Coastal Group of Belfast, she was photographed using her own cranes to load the containers prior to the first sailing on 17 February 1987. The ship is an example of the Type 111a design from the J J Sietas shipyard on the outskirts of Hamburg. She was built as **Sleipner** and delivered to German owners on 6 October 1984. She had been on charter in the West Indies prior to commencing work on the Irish Sea. In late 1988, her charter to Dragon Line ended and she reverted to **Sleipner**. In May 1991 she was renamed **Blue Wave** and the following year was renamed **Rangitoto** for service between New Zealand and Australia. Later changes of name have seen her become **Noumea Express** in 1997 for service between Australia and New Caledonia, and **Bougainville Coast** in 2005 since when she has been trading in Papua New Guinea.

(Bernard McCall)

The scene in Kings Dock on a still 15 November 1986 was very much a blend of old and new. In the distance, two coal hoists can be seen with the **Craigmore** (GBR, 1359gt/66) loading coal for Belfast. Nearer the camera, however, are two coasters with hydraulic wheelhouses that represented the latest in coaster design at that time. Nearest the camera is the **Baursberg** (DEU, 1946gt/83), an example of the Type 100a design from the J J Sietas shipyard. Launched on 10 May 1983, she was delivered on 8 July to Vega Reederei Friedrich Dauber, of Hamburg. In March 1997, she was handed over to other German owners to trade under the Cypriot flag as **Normannia**. By coincidence she had a Welsh connection from May 2005 when she was operated under the Bahamas flag as **Celtic Pride** by Charles Willie (Shipping) Ltd. In 2009, she was acquired by Estonian owners and renamed **Lenglo** under the flag of St Vincent & the Grenadines. The blue-hulled coaster is the **Saimaasee** (DEU, 999grt/82), the second in a series of four sisterships built at the Martin Jansen shipyard in Leer. Launched on 23 October 1982, she was delivered in December. Sold in 1992, she was renamed **Saga** and subsequent changes of identity saw her become **Sarah** (1995), **Trotzenburg** (2000), **Gose Racer** (2005) and, for Italian owners, **Jasmine** since 2009.

(Bernard McCall)

Like all ports, Swansea has handled occasional one-off cargoes such as the heavy-lift seen here in Kings Dock on 15 December 1972. The **Hercules Scan** (DNK, 499grt/71) was built at the Büsum shipyard in northern Germany although her lifting gear was manufactured by Wisbech Refsum and fitted at the Büsum yard. Wisbech Refsum was taken over by Konecranes in 1973. The ship was launched on 8 April 1971 and handed over to Århus-based Blæsbjerg & Co on 22 May. This Danish company specialised in the operation of heavy lift vessels. She was sold out of the fleet in 1979 and was renamed **Biscayne Navco**. On 24 April 1982, she arrived in Hong Kong from Manila. It was reported that she had been sold and was to be renamed **Ashford Bay** but this sale was not completed and she remained laid up in Hong Kong. In mid-1983 she was sold to the People's Republic of China and was renamed **Bei Feng Shan**. She is thought to be still in service.

(John Wiltshire)

15

Briton Ferry is situated almost at the mouth of the River Neath where that river flows into Swansea Bay. An abundance of raw materials found locally combined with the growth of the canal system followed by the rapid expansion of railways in the area ensured that the town developed rapidly during the industrial revolution. Factories were built for the production of iron, steel and tinplate, along with general engineering manufacture. In the mid-20th century, some wharves were used for ship demolition and we see two vessels awaiting their fate. The first is the *Hullgate* (GBR, 1594grt/70), built for the Hull Gates Shipping Co Ltd at the Hessle shipyard of Richard Dunston. The Hull Gates company was taken over by Turnbull Scott in 1981 and shortly after that takeover the *Hullgate* suffered an explosion and serious fire on 23 December 1981 when moored at Amoco's No. 3 berth in Milford Haven. Deemed unworthy of repair, she arrived at Briton Ferry for demolition on 6 February 1982. She was to be scrapped at Neath Abbey wharf and we see her here at Iron Works wharf awaiting suitable tidal conditions to be towed the final two miles.

(W D Harris, Nigel Jones collection)

After World War 2, a wharf on the river was used extensively for the demolition of warships and merchant ships. It is sometimes said that this wharf earned the name Giants Wharf because of the demolition of giant ships but this is incorrect. The names Giants Wharf and Giants Grave had been used in the area for many years prior to World War 2. Awaiting the breakers' torch, the *Deptford* (GBR, 1782grt/51) was another collier built at the Sunderland shipyard of S P Austin & Son. The second of three sisterships, she was launched on 16 August 1951 and delivered to the British Electricity Authority on 27 November. She was another collier of the traditional "flat-iron" design like the *Worthing* on page 10. She retained the same name throughout her career, only the name of the owning company being changed during that time. The British Electricity Authority became the Central Electricity Authority in 1954 and then the Central Electricity Generating Board four years later. The *Deptford* arrived at Briton Ferry for demolition on 6 February 1973 and work began exactly one week later.

(Bob Allen)

In the 1970s, the Mediterranean Shipping Company soon saw the importance of containers for transportation and has since become one of the leading operators of container vessels. The prefix "MSC" is affixed to the names of owned and chartered vessels and it was certainly a surprise to see the **MSC Venture** (ATG, 2446gt/94) at Giants Wharf on 18 March 1999. She had come off charter to the Mediterranean Shipping Company having been employed on a feeder service between Piraeus and Constanta since mid-October 1996. To return her to northern Europe, she loaded reinforcing bars in the Turkish port of Ambarli and arrived at Giants Wharf to discharge her cargo on 17 March. The last vestiges of MSC cream remain on the funnel and clearly "MSC" is about to be removed from her stern. The ship is an example of the hugely successful Rhein class built at the Slovenske Lodenice shipyard at Komarno in Slovakia. Completed as **Lys Trader** in December 1994, she became **MSC Venture** for the duration of the charter already mentioned. She was renamed **Venture** whilst at Giants Wharf and a charter to Seacon saw her become **Sea Severn** between 20 September 2000 and 18 February 2001. Chartered to Norwegian operators in 2002, she was renamed **Wani Venture** and in 2004 she was taken over by the Wilson Group to trade as **Wilson Lista**.

(Bill Moore)

An abbey was established on the western bank of the River Neath by the Cistercians in 1129. By 1730, some of the abbey buildings had been taken over for copper smelting. In the late 18th century an iron foundry was established near the abbey and two furnaces, built in 1792, still survive. A plentiful supply of water and coal, and the proximity of the river for imports and exports, made this an ideal site. It ceased production in the 1880s. The nearby Neath Abbey Wharf has seen many uses and was used extensively for exports of coal until the 1960s. Usage then fell rapidly and in the 1990s, it was used mainly for exports of scrap. In more recent times, it has handled very few vessels indeed. Blue seems to have become the standard hull colour for coasters and there are traces of this still visible beneath the unusual but shabby yellow of the *Duiveland* (NLD, 998gt/83) loading fragmented furnace feed scrap for northern Spain at Neath Abbey Wharf on 1 March 2002. She was launched at the Ferus Smit yard in Foxhol on 7 October 1983 and delivered on 14 December. She was laid up at Ridderkerk on 23 October 2003. Sold at auction in February 2004, she eventually resumed trade as *Antje* in October of that year. In March 2006 she was bought by Italian owners and renamed *Bella* under the flag of St Vincent & the Grenadines. At the time of writing, she trades regularly between ports in Italy and ports on the River Rhône in France.

(Bill Moore)

Lightship No. 72 has a notable history. She was built at Sunderland in 1903 and arrived at Neath Abbey to be scrapped on 30 May 1973. She had been stationed upchannel at the English & Welsh Grounds where she had commenced duty in 1953. Her main claim to fame, however, was her role in marking the approaches to the Mulberry Harbour at the Juno Beach landings during the D-Day invasions. In 1945 she was moved to both the Le Havre and Seine stations to assist the landing of invasion armies. The coaster is the **Fast Sim** (NLD, 1666gt/93), built as **Veritas** at the Peters shipyard in Kampen.

Launched on 3 March 1993, she was delivered on 2 June. Taken on charter by Fast Lines, she became **Fast Sim** in 2001 and four years later was acquired by the Steenstra group in the Netherlands and renamed **Anmar S**. The photograph was taken on 14 July 2002. That year was especially busy with scrap exports from Neath Abbey but the **Fast Sim** was a rare exception as she was loading quarried stone chippings for a wharf on the River Thames.

(Bill Moore)

Opened in 1955, the A48 road bridge over the River Neath allowed traffic linking south-east Wales and west Wales to avoid the lengthy journey via the town of Neath which was the location of the previous crossing. It has provided a good vantage point for ships in the River Neath and we have two views taken from that bridge. Firstly, looking upriver, we see the ***Ingrid*** (CYP, 1960gt/90) outward bound to Calais on the evening tide of 18 September 1998, a gloriously sunny day. She had discharged a cargo of road salt from Kilroot.

Shipyards within the Damen group have continued to be successful in building small vessels. One method of keeping costs down has been to have the hulls of vessels built elsewhere, often in eastern Europe. Other Dutch yards have also been used, however, and it was the De Biesbosch shipyard in Dordrecht that built the hull of the ***Ingrid***. The coaster was completed during March 1990 at the Damen shipyard in Gorinchem. In July 2011, she was sold to Irish operators and renamed ***Florece*** under the flag of Dominica.

(Bill Moore)

Now looking downstream, the **Salvinia** (NLD, 1986gt/86) was starting a voyage to King's Lynn with locally quarried stone chippings when photographed on the afternoon tide of 28 July 2000. This coaster is one of only five low air draught coasters whose construction is credited to the Gebr. Buys shipyard in Krimpen a/d IJssel and the first of three to have a hydraulic wheelhouse. In fact her building details are a little more complex than at first realised. It was her stern section that was launched at the Buys shipyard on 1 October 1986; her fore section was built by Scheepscon at Ouderkerk a/d IJssel. The sections were towed to the Grave shipyard and joined there. She was delivered to Dutch owners as **Alblas** on 22 December 1986 and became **Salvinia** in 1994. Another sale within the Netherlands saw her become **Lammy** in early 2002 but she left Dutch ownership when bought by a German company and renamed **Rova** in December 2009. She is passing the **Arco Dee** which we shall see on page 90.

(Bill Moore)

Our next four photographs depict vessels underway in the river but from different vantage points. There is much of interest to the industrial archaeologist in the Briton Ferry area including the remains of the former dock whose unique lock gate with floating caisson was designed by Sir Marc Brunel, father of Isambard Kingdom Brunel. The accumulator tower providing power to the hydraulic coal tips and three hydraulic cranes in addition to the caisson was been restored and there are ambitious plans to restore the entire dock. The wharf in the background is the appropriately-named Iron Works Wharf. Prominent in the distance is the BP Chemicals plant at Baglan Bay, now demolished. There is more information about these areas on pages 24 - 26. The **Suntis** (DEU, 1564gt/85) is inward bound on 4 September 1987. She is somewhat unusual in having kept her original name for over a quarter of a century following construction at the Hugo Peters shipyard in Wewelsfleth where she was launched on 15 June 1985. She is equipped for the carriage of containers and is strengthened for navigation in ice. Further strengthening allows her not only to carry heavy cargoes but also to be loaded/discharged by grabs.

(Bernard McCall)

By the early 1990s, much road traffic had transferred from the A48 to the M4 but it was increasingly hindered by "the missing link" - a short section of motorway over the River Neath and plans had already been made for the construction of this section. The viaduct over the river, almost 30 metres above high water level, was eventually opened in 1993. The route of this section of motorway had to take account of various industrial, commercial and leisure premises - and a piece of industrial archaeology. The bridge nearer the photographer is the A48 road bridge from which the photographs on the two previous pages were taken. Beyond that is the M4 bridge - no photographs taken from this! To the far right is a gas-fired power station at Baglan Bay. The **Atlantic Sun** (BHS, 1860gt/85) was approaching Giants Wharf to load a cargo of steel coils for Bilbao on 27 June 2002. The ship was launched at Harlingen on 12 March 1985 and delivered as **Waddenzee** on 19 April. She was sold and renamed **Marrow Star** in November 1999 and became **Atlantic Sun** thirteen months later. After five years as such, she was sold to Estonian operators and was renamed **Baltic Sun**, subsequently becoming **Mega** in 2006 and **Tera** in 2007.

(Bill Moore)

The **Delphinus** (DIS, 1793gt/77) makes her approach on Giants Wharf on 23 May 2001 at the end of a voyage from the Swedish port of Luleå with a cargo of manganese ore. She was launched at Harlingen on 28 December 1976 as **Malarsee** and and underwent trials as such but she was delivered on 3 January 1977 as **Norrbotten**. Sold and renamed **IJsselmeer** in 1981, later changes of name saw her become **Fortuna** in 1995, **Klintholm** in 1996 and then **Delphinus** in February 2000. By mid-October 2001 she had changed identity yet again becoming **Blue Ocean** and then, after spending most of August 2003 at Marstal, she was renamed **Gustav** under the Cambodian flag following purchase by Syrian owners.

(Bill Moore)

reinforcing
ja **Marjan**
the River
e evening
in service
livered by
February
2003. Her hull had been built by Ceskoslovenska Plavda Labska at Decin in the Czech Republic. She has remained in Dutch ownership but has had two later names, becoming **Agenor** in March 2005 and **Westewind** in May 2007.

(Bill Moore)

The **Rhone** (GBR, 276grt/66) lies at Iron Works Wharf on 21 May 1988. The explanation for the name of this wharf is on the next page. She began life as a conventional coaster and was launched at Appingedam on 22 September 1966, being handed over to Dutch owners on 29 November. She was converted to a suction dredger after being bought by Llanelli Plant Hire in 1972. She passed through the hands of several owners in South Wales and for a time dredged sea coal in addition to sand. After being laid up in Newport between 1995 and 1997, she was sold to Portuguese owners and traded in the Azores as **Ribeira Grande**. By 2008 she had been renamed **Draga Areia** and had been fitted with a crane. She was scrapped at Horta in the Azores during 2010.

(Bernard McCall)

An iron works was established on the eastern bank of the River Neath in the 1840s and reconstructed in the 1890s. It was closed in 1958 and the site was cleared apart from an engine house, built about 1910, which once contained a Richardson Westgarth quarter crank blowing engine. The engine house is now a Grade II Listed Building. It was constructed of concrete blocks in a steel frame with two rows of classical-style windows. The engine house had to be protected during the construction of the M4 motorway bridge, equally prominent in this view. The bridge deck is supported by eight rows of steel plate girders weighing almost 4000 tons in total. Erection of the central section of the bridge was effected by an 800-ton mobile crane working systematically first from the eastern and then from the western bank. The final sections closing the gap over the river were 60 metres long and weighed 130 tons. Lifting them into their final position over 60 metres from the crane required 400 tons of counterweight. With so much other interest, the **Bure** (PAN, 347gt/69), photographed in early February 1999, seems almost an incidental.

(Bill Moore)

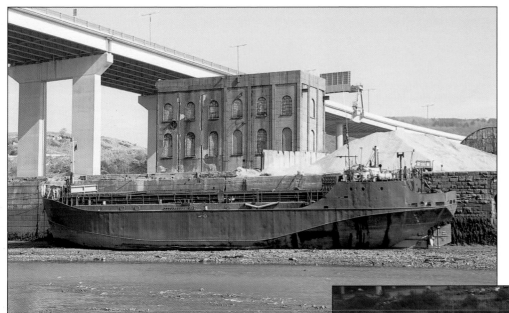

The **Bure** was built as **Cadence** for the London & Rochester Trading Co Ltd (Crescent Shipping) by Drypool Engineering and Dry Dock Co Ltd in Hull. She was sold out of the Rochester fleet in December 1984 and renamed **Bure**. She was transferred to the flag of Panama the following year. In 1995, she came into the ownership of Dalriada Shipping, based in Swansea. In October 1998 she was detained at Corpach and released to sail to Glasgow for temporary repairs before arriving at Iron Works Wharf, Briton Ferry, on 28 January 1999 for permanent repairs. She remained alongside for some three months before returning to the round timber trades in Scotland. She was berthed starboard side to on arrival but by April she was port side to as seen here. By July 2000, however, she was laid up off Castletownbere in the Republic of Ireland and she was eventually demolished in early 2007 at Cahersiveen in County Kerry.

(Bill Moore)

With its refinery at Llandarcy nearby to supply feedstock, in 1963 British Petroleum opened a huge petrochemical plant at Baglan Bay adjacent to the River Neath. Photographed at the Baglan Bay jetty in splendid lighting and at low water on 30 June 1994, the *Sunny Girl* (LBR, 3643gt/89), built at the Hyundai shipyard in Ulsan, South Korea, sits on the river bed as she discharged ethylene from Fawley. In 1995, the *Sunny Girl* was renamed *Happy Girl* and it was on the evening tide of 15 February 2002 that she delivered the final cargo of ethylene from Fawley to Baglan Bay; she departed 24 hours later thus ending a contract on which she had worked for virtually her entire career. After the closure of the Llandarcy refinery in 1998, feedstock had to be imported and this was a factor in the run-down of the Baglan Bay plant which closed in late March 2004. The site was soon totally cleared and became a commercial and business park.

(Bill Moore)

The *Gent* (BEL, 1471gt/79) used to call at Baglan Bay three or four times each year to load diisopropyl ether (DIPE) for Antwerp. DIPE is a by-product of isopropyl which was produced at the plant, isopropyl itself being used in the manufacture of windscreen wash. Beyond the *Gent*, photographed on 22 March 1995, are mounds of sand dredged from the River Neath during the previous month by the *Volvox Anglia* (NLD, 1041gt/80). An annual dredging campaign was needed to remove silt and sand from the turning circle opposite the jetty and the main channel up to the jetty. All the material removed was pumped ashore and used for land reclamation. The *Gent* is an example of the Type 104a design from the J J Sietas shipyard. She was launched on 19 December 1979 and delivered only ten days later as the dry cargo ship *Jan* to Hamburg-based owners. Sold to Belgian owners in January 1987, she was converted to a chemical tanker later that year and renamed *Gent*. Later name changes have seen her become *Eva-H* (March 2001), *Maria* (July 2003) and *Britt* (November 2005).

(Bill Moore)

The letters BGI on the funnel of the *Iida* (EST, 828gt/68) stand for Baltic Group International. She was one of two sister vessels built for Norwegian owners by the H Rancke shipyard at Neuenfelde on the outskirts of Hamburg. She was delivered as *Jolita* in July 1968. In November 1971, she was sold to other Norwegian owners along with sister ship *Joker* and was renamed *Arnholt*. The next three sales saw her remain in Norway, becoming *Citra* in August 1978, *Havblik* in April 1985, and *Siv Hege* in June 1992. In July 1994, she was sold at auction to Estonian buyers. *Lloyd's Register* notes that she was renamed *Ida* before becoming *Iida* but this seems to be incorrect. In 2001 she was sold to operators in Sri Lanka without change of name. She continued to trade in northern Europe until summer 2002. After spending six weeks in Loksa, she left on 19 August and passed south through the Suez Canal on 27 September. By the end of the year, she was trading in south-east Asia mainly between Tuticorin and Colombo. On passage from Tuticorin to Male with building materials, she sank on 29 August 2005 when 37 miles from Tuticorin. Her crew of ten was rescued. Our photograph shows the *Iida* on the morning of 19 August 1999 as she crossed Swansea Bay almost at the end of a voyage from Riga to Port Talbot.

(Danny Lynch)

Aberafan was a small natural harbour at the mouth of the River Afan. A new dock, completed in 1837, is claimed to have been the first major dock to have been built in South Wales and was named after the Talbot family, local landowners. The last quarter of the nineteenth century saw huge improvements and extensions to the dock. We see the *Martinistad* (NLD, 499grt/58) arriving at Port Talbot on 9 May 1969. A typical Dutch coaster of the 1950s, she was built at the Bijlholt shipyard in Foxhol for Dutch owner Dick Kooiman, of Dordrecht. She was launched on 21 September 1957 and delivered on 9 January 1958. In August 1971, she came into British ownership when bought by the West Wales Shipping Co Ltd, of Newport. Subsequent changes of ownership saw her become *Dolphin City* (April 1973), *Hootern* (July 1974) and *River Taw* (September 1976). She had to be towed to Padstow after springing a leak on 9 August 1979 and she departed for Belgium the next day following temporary repairs. In October 1979, however, she was sold for demolition in Kent but almost immediately sold on for further trading in the Caribbean. She was stranded off St Kitts during a tropical storm on 8 September 1981. Although towed to Martinique for temporary repairs, she subsequently sank in Basseterre harbour.

(John Wiltshire)

The **Loke** (DNK, 300grt/70) was launched at the Nordsøværftet shipyard in Ringkøbing on 22 November 1969. She was completed and ready for delivery on 18 February 1970 but ice in the Ringkøbing fjord was so severe that she was unable to leave until 7 April. She was, therefore, relatively new when photographed outward bound from Port Talbot on 14 August 1970. She sank on 5 October 1973 following a collision in the River Weser. After being raised she was taken to Bremen and then towed to Århus in Denmark for permanent repair. She was sold to Faroese owners and renamed **Ocean Trader** in 1982. In mid-July 1988, she loaded explosives at Irvine and, after sailing to Varberg, headed south to Cherbourg and eventually via the Suez Canal to the Far East. In November 1988 she was bought by owners in Singapore and renamed **Hong Soon**. Twelve years later, new owners in Jakarta renamed her **Lian Lestari 5** and she is thought to remain in service as such. In the background of this photograph and that of the **Martinistad** is the funfair on Aberafan beach. Opened in 1963, the funfair was hugely popular and attracted day trippers and holiday makers. In 1966 a huge fire ravaged the restaurant and amusement arcade. Although it was redeveloped during the 1970s, changing leisure patterns resulted in holidaymakers heading for other destinations and in the 1980s, the site became derelict and was cleared. There is a campaign to restore leisure amenities to the area but this is unpopular with the owners and residents of care homes which now line the sea front.

(John Wiltshire)

With the drydock just visible in the left background, the **Kronsberg** (DEU, 712grt/37) enters Port Talbot dock on 9 May 1969. Yet another vessel to have an intriguing history, she began life as a refrigerated cargo ship. She was launched at the Flender Werft shipyard in Lübeck on 24 April 1937 and delivered to the Hamburg-based African Fruit Co as **Porjus** in the following month. On 18 August 1939 she arrived in Hamburg from Gothenburg and was converted to a patrol boat named **V108**. A further conversion saw her re-enter service as **Sperrbrecher 38** in October 1940. The Sperrbrecher ships were converted merchant vessels used by the German navy to escort other vessels through the fairways of defensive minefields into which mines may have strayed. They were also used to clear enemy minefields by simply sailing through them. Inevitably and despite considerable strengthening and the fitting of buoyant material, losses were heavy. The **Sperrbrecher 38**, however, was sunk in a collision off Brunsbüttel on 1 December 1940. She was raised on 27 October 1942 and while being repaired in Hamburg she was severely damaged by bombs on 16 September 1944. She re-entered service as **Sperrbrecher 133** but was sunk yet again off Brunsbüttel, this time by air attack on 6 April 1945. We have been unable to ascertain the date that she was raised but she seems to have been repaired prior to being acquired by B J Schuchmann on 23 September 1949. She was sold to a Greek owner in 1970 and was renamed **Tasso G**. Later becoming **Alkmini** in 1974 and **Vassilakis** in 1975, she was wrecked off the Lebanese coast near Chekka on 27 November 1976.

(John Wiltshire)

29

Port Talbot steelworks was established in 1902 and Margam steelworks in 1916. A consequence was an increase in demand for imports of iron ore, a demand which grew steadily throughout the twentieth century. The dimensions of the entrance lock placed a severe restriction on the size of vessel and in 1966 work started on a new jetty located outside the dock and able to accommodate large bulk carriers. After this opened in 1970, the enclosed dock system closed to commercial vessels. This dock system is extensive and since being reopened for commercial trade in 1998, several wharves have been used. Beneath threatening skies on 21 March 2008, the *Eva Maria Müller* (ATG, 2446gt/98) is about to leave Talbot Wharf after loading a cargo of scrap for Bilbao. This coaster is another example of the Rhein class built at the Slovenske Lodenice shipyard in Komarno. She and sistership *Monika Müller* have spent most of their career so far delivering cement from Santander to Sharpness and taking scrap back to a port in northern Spain either from Sharpness itself or from another Bristol Channel port.

(Bernard McCall)

The enclosed dock at Port Talbot re-opened to commercial shipping in 1998 in order to export ground granulated blast furnace slag (ggbs). This is a cementitious material which is used in the manufacture of concrete, producing a substance that is less permeable and chemically more stable than normal concrete. It is a by-product from the blast furnaces that produce steel. Initially ggbs was taken to the River Thames but a later contract saw supplies being taken to a newly-built import facility at Teignmouth. A regular caller was the

Lass Neptun (DEU, 1513gt/93), photographed loading on 26 August 2006. She was the fourth of five sisterships built at the Rosslauer shipyard on the River Elbe. Launched as **Neptun** on 14 May 1992, she was delivered as **Wolgast** on 6 September 1993 and became **Lass Neptun** the following year. All five vessels were bought by Faversham Ships Ltd and she was renamed **Valiant** in 2008.

(Bernard McCall)

In addition to berths within the enclosed docks, the entrance lock at Port Talbot is also used for cargo handling. Various commodities have been handled at this location including ggbs which is taken to Purfleet or Glasgow generally by ships in the fleet of Aasen Transport such as the **Aasnes** (NIS, 3136gt/81) which was loading for Glasgow on 17 May 2007. The ship was built by Svendborg Skibsværft and completed in May 1981 as **Medallion** for Danish owners. She was sold in 2002 to Aasen Transport, a Norwegian company which specialises in the transport of bulk cargoes and whose ships are fitted with self-discharge gear. The **Aasnes** was refitted for such work when bought in 2002 and she is equipped with a Hitachi ZX650 excavator.

(Bernard McCall)

It was in 2007 that the enclosed dock at Port Talbot saw the first imported cargo of steel since the 1960s. In April 2010, two vessels were worked simultaneously in the lock for the first time. The **Nautica** (VCT, 1587gt/92) was discharging 1500 tonnes of steel reinforcing bars for Dyfed Reinforcement. She was launched at the Ferus Smit shipyard in Foxhol on 20 June 1992 and delivered on 10 August as **Vesting**. Later name changes saw her become **Meander** (2000) and **Nautica** (2005). The **Fast Sus** (BEL, 2055gt/96) was also built in the north of the Netherlands but at the Barkmeijer shipyard in Stroobos. Launched as **Aletis** on 15 March 1996, she was handed over to Dutch owners on 16 April. She became **Fast Sus** when chartered by Fast Lines in 1999 and was bought by this company in 2007. She was discharging 2900 tonnes of steel scrap to be used in the huge Tata Steel UK facility alongside the dock. This will be better known as the Margam steelworks of British Steel, and later Corus.

(Robert Cutforth, Associated British Ports)

We now leave the western section of our survey and go round Nash Point to see the ports in south-east Wales. At anchor in Barry Roads on 21 August 1976 is the *Hoofort* (GBR, 446grt/65). She was built by the Ailsa Shipbuilding Co Ltd at Troon and was launched on 5 January 1964. In January of the following year, she was handed over to the Isle of Man Steam Packet Co Ltd as *Ramsey* for that company's cargo services to the Isle of Man. With more and more cargo being unitised, she was sold out of the Manx fleet in 1974 and acquired by R Lapthorn & Co Ltd by whom she was renamed **Hoofort**. In 1982, she was sold to owners in the Cape Verde islands and was renamed *Boa Entrada*. She was converted to a tanker in 1987 and two years later was sold to other Cape Verde owners for trading as *Arquipelago*. She is still listed in *Lloyd's Register*.

(Nigel Jones)

We try to avoid using photographs of vessels that have appeared in earlier volumes in this series but we make an exception for this perfectly-lit image of the *Eileen M* (GBR, 870grt/66) as she arrives at Barry on the evening tide of 21 October 1972, no doubt to load a cargo of coal. This would possibly be delivered to Yelland in North Devon or Hayle in Cornwall, and it was in *Coasters of Cornwall* that we first saw this vessel as she loaded stone at Porthoustock. Built by the Burntisland Shipbuilding Co Ltd for Metcalf Motor Coasters, she was launched on 19 April 1966 and delivered in July. Lengthened by 37 feet (11,27 metres) in 1977, she was sold seven years later

to operators in the Caribbean and on 30 September 1984 left Teignmouth for Barbados. It was claimed that she would be renamed *Celt Pioneer* but she traded under her original name for two years before arriving at the Colombian port of Mamonal on 11 April 1986. She was then laid up with surveys overdue and supposedly under repair. At this time, reports said she had been renamed *Caerleon* but she never traded as such and she was still called *Eileen M* when she returned to service in late March 1988. She is yet another vessel whose ultimate fate is currently unknown.

(Nigel Jones)

Seen from Barry's eastern breakwater, the *Mossville* (GBR, 499grt/53) heads towards the lock on 6 August 1969. The hill in the background is known as Nell's Point and clearly visible is the Butlin's holiday camp which, despite fierce local opposition, had opened there three years previously. It was the last of the Butlin's camps to be built and was the smallest although it had over 800 chalets and could accommodate 5000 people. Its closure was announced in 1986 and, bought by other owners, it struggled on for a further decade. Since 1996, the site has been gradually cleared and, just as controversially, has been used for housing. The *Mossville* was built at the Voorwaarts shipyard in Martenshoek. She was launched on 8 November 1952 and delivered to her original Groningen-based owner as *Meteoor* in January 1953. She did not remain long under the Dutch flag for in 1954 she was bought by Ald Shipping, of Bristol, and renamed *Castle Combe*. In 1960 she was sold and renamed *Mossville*. She left northern Europe for the eastern Mediterranean when bought by owners in Syria and renamed *Anastasia* in 1972. Renamed *Omar* in 1983, she was scrapped in Lattakia three years later.

(Nigel Jones)

The **Seefeldersand** (DEU, 999grt/69) had just left the lock at Barry and was outward bound in July 1973. The cranes visible in the distance to the right of the photograph are on the south side of No. 2 Dock. Owned by Brake-based Helmut Meyer, the **Seefeldersand** was the second of seven sisterships built for the company in an order that was shared by two shipyards. She was launched at the C Lühring yard in Brake on 22 May 1969 and delivered on 10 June. All the ships in the Meyer fleet had a purposeful appearance but were not suited to changing patterns of trade in the early 1980s. She was laid up at Bremerhaven on 8 June 1982 along with four other ships in the fleet.

When eventually sold to Yugoslavian owners in September 1983 and renamed **Gradina**, she was the final vessel to leave the Meyer fleet. Later sales saw her become **Vale** in 1992 and then **Babs** and **Ahmad J** in 1993. On 28 June 1994 she grounded on the coast of Cyprus when on passage from Izmail to Tripoli (Lebanon). She refloated with tug assistance and was repaired at Limassol. A sale in 1997 saw her become **Oula Queen** and she eventually sank on 16 March 2001 when on passage from Novorossiysk to Syria with a grain cargo. Eight of her crew of eleven were rescued by a Russian ship.

(Bob Allen)

The **Tanja Holwerda** (NLD, 938gt/76) loads scrap in Barry's No. 3 Dock Basin on 3 July 1984. In the mid-1980s, the buildings in the background were swept away so that a new terminal could be built for Geest Line whose refrigerated vessels had returned to Barry after a brief sojourn in Avonmouth. The ship is one of a class of eight distinctive vessels constructed at the Barkmeier shipyard in Stroobos. She began life as **Roelof Holwerda**, being renamed **Tanja Holwerda** in 1981, and remained in Holwerda ownership even after transfer to the Cypriot flag in 1987 when she became **The Dutch**. On 27 July 1987, she encountered heavy weather off the east coast of England when on passage from Archangel to Boston with a cargo of timber. She was abandoned by her crew, salvaged by United Towing and eventually declared a constructive total loss. Bought by J R Rix, she underwent extensive repairs and lengthening in Hull's Central Drydock. Renamed **Magrix**, she re-entered service and, sold to other British owners in 1998, became **Nicky L**. The following year she was acquired by Dutch operators and transferred to the flag of Belize as **Abalone**. She then departed for the Caribbean. She arrived in tow at George Town, Cayman Islands, on 2 March 2004 with machinery damage. On 6 May she was towed to Belize City for discharge of part of her steel cargo and then on to Tampico for discharge of the remainder and assessment of damage. She seems to have been repaired and switched to the flag of Mexico in October 2004 but there are no further details.

(Bernard McCall)

In early 2006, the British government offered a subsidy to power generators in order to persuade them to reduce emissions by using palm oil instead of fuel oil. Several cargoes of palm oil were delivered to Barry and were discharged direct to road tanker in No. 3 dock. The **Ellen Theresa** (IOM, 1734gt/83) was discharging palm oil from Rotterdam when photographed on 5 May 2006. She was launched at the Meltem shipyard in Beykoz on the outskirts of Istanbul on 12 November 1982. The building of product tankers in Turkey has developed considerably during the ensuing three decades. She was built for German owners as **Regina** and but was renamed **Cisca** shortly after delivery. In 1986 she entered the fleet of Hamburg-based Reederei-Atlantic F & W Joch whose tankers were named after Indian tribes in North America. She became **Cheyenne**, a name she retained for fourteen years until becoming part of the fleet of Herning Tankers. This Danish company renamed her **Ellen Theresa**. A sale to Russian operators in 2007 saw her renamed **Ellen** for a brief period of trade between the Mediterranean and Sea of Azov but in 2008 she was bought by owners in Colombia and arrived at Cartagena in late February. Later in the year, she was renamed **San Andres II**.

(Nigel Jones)

Above : The first dock to be built in Barry was No. 1 Dock which opened on 18 July 1889. It was the brainchild of David Davies, a railway contractor and colliery owner who shared the concern of other colliery owners in the Rhondda, Ogmore and Llynfi valleys when the Bute Docks company in Cardiff planned to increase rates by one penny per ton. The dock was an immediate success with three millions tons of coal exported in the first year, rising to a peak of over eleven million tons in 1913. In its later years, No. 1 Dock was used for imports of sand and exports of scrap but mainly for the import of chemicals and petroleum products ranging from motor spirit to molasses and coal tar. Looking eastwards along No. 1 Dock on 21 November 1971, we see the *Elizabeth Broere* (NLD, 594grt/67) awaiting departure. She was launched at the J G Hitzler shipyard in Lauenburg on 20 July 1967 and delivered to Gebr. Broere on 19 October. In February 1971, she was lengthened by 9,65 metres at the De Groot & van Vliet shipyard in Slikkerveer. She was sold to Greek owners and renamed *Olympia* in 1984 and became *Anastasios I* in 2002. Renamed *Sofia* in July 2010, she arrived for demolition at Aliaga only two months later.

(John Wiltshire)

Right : The *Coenraad-K* (NLD, 454grt/58) is typical of hundreds of coasters built in the Netherlands in the 1950s. She was launched by Scheepswerf & Reparatiebedrijf "Harlingen" on 22 June 1958 and delivered on 30 August to her Harlingen-based owner. A sale within the Netherlands in November 1974 saw her renamed *Rosa-B* under the flag of Panama. She continued to trade in northern Europe and it was not until April 1978 that she left the area for the eastern Mediterranean following sale to Syrian owners by whom she was renamed *Rizk Allah*. Renamed *Walid* in 1985 and *Mariam* the following year, she survived only until early 1988 when she arrived at Gadani Beach for demolition. She awaits loading at a coal hoist in No. 1 Dock on 15 March 1970. In the 1940s, Barry had thirty coal hoists. Not a single one has been preserved either here or in any Welsh port. All that remains in Barry are the plinths on which the hoists stood.

(Nigel Jones)

The **Oarsman** (GBR, 1550gt/79) approaches the lock from No. 1 Dock on 13 August 1994. She was built at the Hessle shipyard of Richard Dunston, situated a few miles west of Hull on the northern bank of the River Humber. Launched on 18 October 1979 she was delivered to C Rowbotham & Sons (Management) Ltd in January of the following year. In 1974, the Dunston yard had come into the ownership of the Ingram Corporation and the Rowbotham company later acted as technical advisers and managers for two of that company's tankers. Over the next two decades, ownership of the **Oarsman** passed to various companies including the P&O Group, whose colours she is wearing in this photograph, and then James Fisher & Sons PLC. In 2003, she left the UK coast for warmer climes having been sold to owners in Malta by whom she was renamed **Anchor Bay** and was used mainly for bunkering work. The area in the background now bears little resemblance to that seen here. It is the location of the "Waterfront", a large residential and commercial area of redevelopment.

(Nigel Jones)

The **Baltic Prosperity** (PAN, 2270grt/65) has been involved in various unfortunate incidents during her career. She was built by Lödöse Varf, a shipyard located on the Göta Älv north of Gothenburg. She was launched on 2 February 1965 and delivered as **Luna** on 28 June to Swedish tanker operator OT-Rederierna. Sold within Sweden in 1974, she was renamed **Bellona** but in December of that year she was acquired by Irish owners and renamed **Rathowen**. On 25 September 1981, she was towed to Valletta after water ingress into her engine room when on passage from Tarragona to Salahar. She departed for Tarragona on 4 January 1982 and arrived in Barry to lay up on 31 March. It was reported at the time that she had 200 tons of solid bitumen in her tanks. Be that as it may, she found a buyer and was renamed **Baltic Prosperity**, a strange choice of name for a vessel that was to sail to West Africa and thence to trade in the South Atlantic, usually delivering marine gas oil from Montevideo to fishing vessels working around the Falkland Islands. She left Barry on 18 September 1983. Whilst at anchor in Berkeley Sound on 18 December 1996, fire broke out and her accommodation was gutted. Her cargo was transferred to a Russian tanker and she was towed to Montevideo for inspection, arriving on 2 January 1997.

Arguably of more interest than the tanker is the large building in the background. This was the dock office of the Barry Docks Company and is a fine example of Victorian architecture. It was brainchild of Arthur Bell, a Cardiff architect, who based his design on the annual calendar. Consequently the building has 4 floors, 52 fireplaces, 12 panels and 7 lights in the entrance porch, 365 windows, 31 steps to each floor, and 2 circular windows representing the sun and the moon. It also has two sets of stairways, a wide marble one at the front and a narrow concrete one at the back. During the time of the Barry Docks Company, all staff had to use the narrow stairs whilst the directors used the wide marble ones. The clock was installed by William Potts & Sons, of Leeds, and its mechanism was started on 5 December 1899. In 1984, it suffered a disastrous fire but it was renovated by Associated British Ports. In 1995, the building was taken over by the Vale of Glamorgan Council. At the time, a large safe on the ground floor was used for storing impounded drugs. It is appropriate that in front of the building stands a statue of David Davies.

(Bernard McCall)

Barry has always been a popular port for laying up vessels and over the last four decades has seen a wide variety of ships laid up including Blue Star cargo ships and BP tankers. We now move to Barry's No. 2 Dock to see the **Booker Talisman** (NLD, 499grt/60) which was laid up during the winter of 1973/74. She was launched by Terneuzensche Scheepsbouw Mij. in Terneuzen on 25 July 1960 and in October of that year was delivered as **Ria** to owners in nearby Breskens. After a decade as such, she entered the fleet of Liverpool-based S William Coe but was registered in Bridgetown, Barbados. This company was a subsidiary of the Booker Line, established in 1835 to carry sugar from the West Indies and Guyana, and the **Ria** was renamed **Booker Talisman**. Four years later, she was acquired by the Atlantic Levant Line and transferred to the Lebanese flag as **Beit Mery**, becoming **Borealis** on transfer to the Cypriot subsidiary of Atlantic Levant Line in 1976. That name proved to be short-lived as she was wrecked off Magna in the Gulf of Aqaba when on passage in ballast from Haqi to Limassol on 1 October 1976.

(Nigel Jones)

In addition to the storage of bananas, the cold store on No 2 Dock was used for Egyptian potatoes. The **Polly Polaris** (BHS, 1528grt/70), seen on 7 March 1991, had arrived the previous day with potatoes and fruit from Alexandria. She was launched at the Groningen yard of Nieuwe Noord Nederlandsche Scheepswerven on 31 October 1969. Built as **Leo Polaris** for a local owner, she was soon taken on charter by Seatrade Groningen, a company which was formed in 1951 by five captain-owners and which decided to specialise in refrigerated vessels a decade later. This vessel formed part of the company's rapid expansion programme in the mid-1970s. In July 1984 she was sold to Bahamas-flag operators and was renamed **Diamond Despina**, becoming

Polly Polaris four years later. She was one of several refrigerated vessels acquired in the late 1980s as part of the meteoric growth of Polly Peck International (PPI). By 1990, this company, with interests in textiles and electronics, had joined Chiquita, Dole and Del Monte as the leading companies in the fresh fruit and vegetable trades in western Europe and North America. In less than a decade PPI's capitalisation grew from £300,000 to £1.7 billion. The fall was just as quick - but that is another story. The **Polly Polaris** was sold to owners in Thailand in 1991 and was renamed **IMG 3**. Sold within Thailand in May 2010, she became **Silver Sea 3**.

(Bernard McCall)

It was in 1875 that Joseph Rank began to mill corn using steel rollers instead of millstones. The mill on the south side of No. 2 Dock was built in 1905 thanks to incentives from the Barry Railway Company which provided a loan of £40,000 for building costs and a low rental lease for 250 years. The mill suffered a serious fire in 1912 but was rebuilt. Amongst the branded flour produced was "Ocean Pride" for the Royal Navy and shipping companies, and "Banzai" for the Japanese market. Animal feedstuffs were also produced. The products were bagged in sacks made of Egyptian cotton and these were popular with the ladies who worked in the mill. The cotton could be washed and used to make tablecloths petticoats and knickers. A large section of the mill was demolished in 1990. The **Nordsaga** (DEU, 999grt/64) has the distinction of being the only Type 45 coaster from the J J Sietas shipyard. She was launched on 8 September 1964 and delivered to her original Hamburg-based owner as **Inga Sabine** on 4 October 1964. In June 1974, she was sold within Germany and renamed **Nordsaga**. This photograph was taken on19 April 1983 and by this stage in her career she had lost her midships mainmast and two of her four 3-tonne cranes. Later in that year owner Hans-Otto Gadermann renamed her **Sabina**. There was a further variation on her original name when she became **Inga-B** following a sale in 1986. In 1990, she was sold to Caribbean operators without change of name but her two remaining cranes were removed and replaced by an NCK Rapier lattice crane fixed amidships.

(Bernard McCall)

The **Ashington** (GBR, 4334grt/79) has discharged her cargo of cement and is negotiating the passage from No. 2 Dock to No. 1 Dock as she begins a voyage to Boulogne on 21 August 1988. She was launched at the Wallsend shipyard of Clelands on 14 December 1978 and delivered to Stephenson Clarke in April of the following year. Earlier in 1988 she had been fitted with computer-controlled wingsails that were fitted above her bridge and these had been removed not long before this photograph was taken. There were mixed reports about the success of the wingsails although it was clear that fuel savings were made. Her master reckoned an average of 8% savings during the period of the trial, a figure which improved as far as 20% under certain conditions. The experiment also showed that significant engine modifications would be required if the design were to be a commercial success. The ship was sold to Norwegian operators and renamed **Fjord Pearl** in late November 2004, becoming **JP Fox** in September 2007. One year later, she was acquired by Egyptian owners and started to trade in the Mediterranean and Black Sea as **Milano Star**.

(Bernard McCall)

At the eastern end of No. 2 Dock is 31 Berth. In the 1980s this was used by bulk carriers importing pumice from the Greek island of Yali. It was also used by coasters loading scrap and handling cargoes of cement. Cement clinker exports started in 1983 and ended four years later, but that same commodity was imported from 1988. The **Arklow Glen** (IRL, 993grt/79), photographed on 29 January 1989, was launched at the Bijlholt shipyard in Foxhol on 18 May 1979 and delivered as **Tromp** to Dutch owners on 4 July. Laid up in 1982 following the financial collapse of her owners, she was taken over by a bank and she came into the Arklow Shipping fleet as **Arklow Glen** in August 1984. She remained with the Irish company for a decade before being sold to Norwegian owners and renamed **Fortuna**. In 2006, she was bought by owners in the Faroe Islands and renamed **Havfrakt**.

(Bernard McCall)

Even in the mid-1970s, there was a degree of optimism about solid fuel exports through Barry and in 1978, a new coal/coke loader was brought into use which had a capacity of 450 tons per hour. Bulk carriers loaded notably for Romania whilst coasters loaded for Sweden, Germany, Ireland and the Channel Islands. The **Commodity** (GBR, 582gt/75) was reported to be loading for the latter when photographed after a heavy storm on 29 January 1984. She was the first of two sisterships and was launched at the Wivenhoe shipyard of J W Cook & Co on 10 July 1975 with delivery to F T Everard two months later. She remained in the Everard fleet until late 1993 when she was sold to Scottish owners without change of name. She spent much time delivering malting barley to Port Ellen on the island of Islay and also to ports in north-east Scotland such as Burghead, Buckie and Macduff, a trade for which she had been designed. Although the identity of her owners changed during the ensuing twelve years, she was not renamed until 2005 when she became **Lina F** for trade under the flag of North Korea for owners believed to be Syrian. The following year saw her renamed **Sea Doll** and then she became **Safe M** in 2007. On 14 December 2008 she sank in heavy weather five miles from the Libyan coast off Marsa el Brega while on passage from Larissa to Sfax with sand. Her crew was rescued.

(Bernard McCall)

Again at the eastern end of No 2 Dock but on the south side and opposite No. 31 berth, there is a chemical berth which has handled a wide variety of chemicals for the large petrochemical complexes in the area, notably European Vinyls Corporation Ltd and Dow Corning for whom Vopak offers storage facilities. The *Haugvik* (NIS, 1599grt/73) was built at the J Pattje shipyard in Waterhuizen. Launched on 26 June 1973, she was delivered as *Sigurd Jorsalfar* on 7 November to Einar Bakkevig, of Oslo. Sold within Norway in 1985, she was renamed *Haugvik* and is seen discharging vinyl chloride monomer from Porsgrunn on 20 May 1991. On 26 July 1997, she departed northern Europe, leaving Le Havre for Cuba, and she then traded in the Caribbean for two years until in July 1999 she was sold to Peruvian operators for trading mainly between Callao and Talara under the Panamanian flag as *Escorpio Gas* from early September. A report that she became *Farhan* in July 2007 may be inaccurate - she seems to have arrived at Callao as *Escorpio Gas* in November 2007. She appears to have been laid up then with surveys overdue and class suspended. The next report suggests that she arrived at Alang for demolition on 6 July 2008. That was not the end of her career, though. In 2009, the Vishwakarma Maritime Institute established a one year postgraduate course in marine engineering and bought the partly-demolished ship to allow students to gain practical experience during their studies.

(Bernard McCall)

We move east from Barry and look at the approaches to Cardiff. In Cardiff's residential suburb of Penarth, there used to be three excellent vantage points for watching ships going to and from Cardiff or, at a greater distance, Newport and Avonmouth. At sea level, one had a choice of Penarth pier or the nearby beach. By far the best vantage point, however, was Penarth Head where there was a break in the residential development that allowed an unrestricted view of ships in the Wrach Channel. The ***Esso Tenby*** (GBR, 2170gt/70) passes Penarth Head on 16 April 1992 almost at the end of a voyage from Milford Haven with a cargo of fuel oil. She was launched by Appledore Shipbuilders

on 3 October 1970 and delivered the following month. The first of three sisterships from this yard, each was intended for a different purpose and the ***Esso Tenby*** was designed for the carriage of heavy black oils to oil-fired power stations although she carried a wider variety of cargoes later in her career. In 1994, she was sold to Hull-based John H Whitaker (Tankers) Ltd and was renamed ***Whitcrest***. She arrived at Birkenhead to be laid up in mid-August 2002 and eventually departed for Nigeria in late 2003. It was reported that she had been renamed ***Pavilion*** by 2005 but nothing further is known of her.

(Bernard McCall)

A second view from the vantage point at the end of Penarth Head Lane. The origins of the **Navaro** (DEU, 999grt/84) are unusual to say the least. She was a silver wedding gift to themselves by owners Hubert and Erna Schepers whose family is one of several significant coaster operators based in the town of Haren on the River Ems. Built at the Martin Jansen shipyard in Leer, the ship was christened by their daughter Elke at noon on 5 May 1984, exactly 25 years after the couple were married. The ship was handed over in June and sailed to Archangel where she loaded packaged timber for the Mediterranean on her first commercial voyage. It was expected that her usual cargoes would be timber such as that seen here being delivered to Cardiff on 22 August 1987. Evident on her port side are two 8-tonne cranes; these were removed in 1995. Two years prior to that she had been sold to Captain Rudolf Schepers and renamed **Svendborg**. She was acquired by Estonian owners in 2004 and renamed **Agat**.

(Bernard McCall)

The construction of the barrage across Cardiff Bay has provided another excellent vantage point for watching ships as they sail to or from the port of Cardiff. Outward bound to Rotterdam on 3 August 2004 is the **Marjola** (LTU, 2061gt/81). She was launched at the Rauma-Repola shipyard in Uusikaupunki on 14 November 1980 and delivered as **Pohjola** in February of the following year. Finnish shipyards have been prolific in building for other countries but not for Finland where shipowning has been hampered by restrictive rules and regulations. This vessel was one of a class of seven.

Three were built for Russia and four for Finland of which two were for the builders' own account. The **Pohjola** was the second of these two. Although ideally suited for the Baltic timber trades, the ship was too expensive to operate and was laid up at Uusikaupunki on 17 July 1983. Sold in 1984, she had a succession of owners and names before becoming **Marjola** in 1996. Ownership has been more settled since she was acquired by a Russian operator and renamed **Poline** in 2005.

(Bernard McCall)

The **Coastal Breeze** (ATG, 1934gt/78) was built at the Nobiskrug shipyard in Rendsburg. She was launched on 21 November 1978 and delivered as **Eider** on 29 December. A popular feeder vessel, she was chartered by Team Lines for its routes from Hamburg to Norway and Sweden. On 25 July 1994, she arrived at the Naval Shipyard in Gdynia where she was lengthened by 15,5 metres, increasing her container capacity from 142TEU to 178TEU. She returned to service on 31 August. In 1998, she ceased feeder work and commenced general cargo trade. It was in late January 2002 that she was chartered by Coastal Container Line, a wholly-owned subsidiary of the Mersey Docks & Harbour Board, and renamed **Coastal Breeze**. Coastal Container Line was established to link Liverpool to Belfast and Dublin with occasional calls at Cardiff and the **Coastal Breeze** was arriving from Dublin when photographed as she approached Cardiff on 16 May 2004. She reverted to her original name in summer 2007 and, although remaining initially on the CCL service, she had returned to general trade by the end of the year.

(Nigel Jones)

Space precludes a detailed history of Penarth Dock. Suffice it to say that where once ships used to be loaded with coal, there is now a marina and residential development. The approach to the locks which give access to the marina needs regular dredging. This is often entrusted to the **Sospan** (PAN, 718gt/90) which was built at the Slob shipyard in Papendrecht and is owned by the Royal Boskalis Group in the Netherlands. This family-owned dredging company obtained work in the UK in the early 1930s and thought it wise to establish an associated company in the UK. So it formed Westminster Dredging, deeming that such a title would appeal to potential customers in the UK. Llanelli Sand Dredging was formed as an offshoot to dredge aggregates off the coast of West Wales and operates two dredgers. The name **Sospan** which, in Welsh, means "Saucepan", recalls Llanelli's traditional connection with the tinplate industry, tinplate being used in the manufacture of such kitchen items. The photograph was taken on 8 August 2006 and looks towards the three locks which give access to Cardiff Bay and Penarth Marina. To the right are the sluices controlling the water level in the Bay. The River Taff and the River Ely flow into the bay and the barrage also has fish gates which allow salmon to enter the Bay in order to reach breeding grounds in the Taff. In the far distance to the right is the Millennium Stadium.

(Bernard McCall)

Ely Tidal Harbour opened in 1859, six years before Penarth Dock. The banks of the River Ely were soon lined with coal hoists with the final coal exports being taken in the 1960s. The last operational berth in the Ely river served an Esso terminal and closed officially on 14 September 1985, the distribution of Esso products having been transferred to Avonmouth. In the 1930s, there were two large depots for petroleum products, one operated by the Anglo-American Oil Company and the other by National Benzole. The **Esso Dover** (GBR, 490grt/61), entering the River Ely in July 1970, was launched at the Poole shipyard of J Bolson & Son on 19 December 1960 and delivered to the Esso Petroleum Co Ltd in March 1961. In 1980 she was sold to Tees-based operators and renamed **Cherrybobs**. Later in that same year, she was sold to the St Helena Shipping Company and renamed **Bosun Bird**. She sailed to the South Atlantic where her new role was to load fuel at Ascension for the island of St Helena where she would lie as a floating fuel store. Her cargo was used to bunker the **St Helena** which served the island from Europe, and also provided domestic fuel for the island. She had the distinction of being featured on the St Helena 45p stamp commemorating the 300th anniversary of the settlement of the island. She was renamed **Alreen** in 1992 following sale to owners in Mombasa and was reported to have been scrapped there during the Summer of 2001 although some sources suggest that demolition came later.

(Bob Allen)

The **Ludwig** (CYP, 1209gt/69) was one of the most
frequent callers to the Esso berth in Ely tidal harbour in
the early 1980s and was noted on 14 November 1982.
Not having a bow thruster, she always required tug
assistance when berthing. She was the first of three
sisterships built at the Krögerwerft shipyard at Schacht-
Audorf on the Kiel Canal near Rendsburg for Hamburg-
based owner Leth & Co to whom she was delivered on
30 May 1969. All three were lengthened by 11,8 metres
at the Jos L Meyer shipyard in Papenburg, the **Ludwig**
being modified in December 1974. She was sold to
Greek owners in 1995 and renamed **Taxiarchis I**,
moving on to operators in Dubai under the name **Sama**
two years later. Nothing has been heard of her since
2009. Although it is likely that the area would have
ultimately been redeveloped as it has during the last two
decades, the immediate reason for the closure of the oil
terminal was a new tax regime which related to oil
storage - see also page 59.

(Bernard McCall)

The **BP Warrior** (GBR, 1410gt/68) was one of several
coastal tankers built in the late 1960s to distribute oil
products for Shell Mex & BP, a joint marketing enterprise
established in 1932. All of the tankers had the names of
Shell or BP refineries or distribution depots and this
vessel was launched at the Hall, Russell shipyard in
Aberdeen as **Grangemouth** on 25 April 1968. When the
Shell Mex & BP joint agreement came to an end in the
mid-1970s, the fleet was divided between the two
constituent companies and the **Grangemouth** was
renamed **BP Warrior**. In 1997, she became **Border
Warrior** as a consequence of internal reorganisation
within BP. She spent much of her career delivering
products from BP's Grangemouth refinery to ports in
eastern and northern Scotland. She arrived at
Grangemouth for the final time on 6 July 2004. She was
de-stored and departed six days later for Santander
where ahe arrived for demolition on 17 July. Her arrival at
the Esso terminal on the River Ely on 15 August 1983 was
certainly worthy of note.

(Bernard McCall)

Before the construction of a barrage across Cardiff Bay, sea-dredged sand was discharged at a wharf near the mouth of the River Taff adjacent to Ferry Road in Grangetown. In the latter years, this wharf was served exclusively by the **Bowqueen** (GBR, 1317grt/63) which is seen approaching the wharf on 25 May 1987. She was launched at the Troon yard of Ailsa Shipbuilding Company on 29 November 1962 and was delivered in February 1963 to British Dredging. Initially she worked on the Thames and off the coast of Essex and it was when off Orford Ness that she suffered a tragedy when she heeled over and sank on 8 September 1965. The Master, his wife and a Maltese crewman were lost in the accident which was caused by the vessel having been badly loaded. In 1988, she was sold to Portuguese owners for trading out of Funchal on the island of Madeira. She was renamed **Susana Cristina** under the flag of Portugal.

(Bob Allen)

We now have five images of ships near the entrance lock at Cardiff. The *City of Southampton* (GBR, 1097gt/69) was built by Appledore Shipbuilders and was launched as *Hoveringham V* on 27 June 1969 with completion coming in September of that year. She was lengthened by 8,5 metres in 1973. Originally owned by Hoveringham, this company was taken over by Tarmac plc in 1981 and it was on 22 October of that year that the *Hoveringham V* had the distinction of being the last commercial vessel to sail from the port of Preston prior to the port's formal closure nine days later. In 1989, she was renamed *City of Southampton* when she was taken over by United Marine Dredging. In 1997, she was sold to Greek owners and was renamed *Leon I*, becoming *Kavonissi* the following year and *Elefantas* in 2004. We see her approaching Cardiff on the morning of 15 August 1994. In the background to the right of the image can be seen the lock gates of Penarth Marina and some of the modern buildings constructed on the site of the former coal exporting dock. The two grey buildings to the left are of interest, both being Grade II listed. On the right is the Custom House, also dating from 1865, whose clock tower bears the royal coat-of-arms. It has now been refurbished and houses two restaurants. On the left is the former Marine Hotel, built by the Taff Vale Railway and having the TVR logo on the wrought iron balcony balustrades. It has been derelict since 1973.

(Nigel Jones)

We now pan right to see the *Koriangi* (RUS, 1598gt/93) arriving at Cardiff on 17 May 1998. In the early 1990s, a complex series of transactions saw two Russian companies acquire a major share in the Cassens shipyard in Emden. One of these companies was the White Sea Onega Shipping Company which placed an order for five coasters with Arminius Werke at Bodenwerder, far inland on the River Weser and another associated company. To meet tight delivery dates, one of the five was subcontracted to the Cassens yard and a sixth vessel was added to the order, to be built at Emden. This sixth vessel was the *Koriangi* which was launched on 6 August 1993 and delivered later in that same month. Prominent in the middle distance is a temporary causeway built as part of the construction work for the barrage across Cardiff Bay. Beyond are more residential buildings around Penarth Marina. In its heyday, Penarth Dock was lined with coal loading hoists. It is worth recording that over four million tons of coal was exported from Penarth Dock in 1913. The skyline in the distance is dominated by a controversial housing estate built in the 1960s and now demolished. Known locally as the Bilibanks, the name is believed to be a shortened version of Bilberry Banks, bilberry bushes having grown abundantly on the slopes from pre-Victorian times and raided each autumn by local residents wishing to make fruit pies.

(Nigel Jones)

In the late afternoon and evening, the northern side of the lock approach was ideal for photography. Sadly, the twin issues of security and health & safety have made viewpoints such as this inaccessible to the general public. On the cloudless summer evening of 2 August 1996, the *Sea Weser* (ATG, 1939gt/83) approaches the lock with Penarth Head in shadow in the background. She is an example of the standard Type 110 design from the J J Sietas shipyard and was launched as *Jenika* in December 1982. Having been chartered by Seacon, she was delivered to German owners as *Sea Weser* on 28 January 1983. A sale within Germany saw her renamed *Treuburg* in 1999 and, bought by Norwegian operators in 2004, she became *Stabben Junior*.

(Nigel Jones)

The photographer was standing on a tidal oil berth just outside the lock entrance as the fully-laden **Carebeka III** (NLD, 963grt/64) emerged from the lock in June 1973. The Carebeka company was an association of Dutch captain-owners established in 1939 in order to obtain freight contracts on the best possible terms. It became one of the four leading companies of its kind in the Netherlands. In the 1950s, it expanded into ship ownership and this ultimately led to its bankruptcy in 1983. Building ships required capital that had to be raised by loans, often at a high interest rate, and this was a very different matter from looking after the commercial interests of captain-owners. The **Carebeka III** was launched at the J Pattje shipyard in Waterhuizen on 3 July 1964 and delivered to Carebeka on 20 November. In late 1969, she was lengthened by 7,16 metres at the Niestern shipyard in Groningen. Sold and renamed **Albert Cornelis** in 1981, she became **Lane** in 1983 and **Lang** in 1988. Later in 1988, she was bought by American owners for trading in the Caribbean as **Rebeka**. Arriving at Mamonal, Colombia, for repair on 6 March 1991, she was later abandoned by her owners. She eventually sank at Mamonal on 19 February 1998, and was later raised and scrapped.

(Bob Allen)

Like the **Oarsman** on page 40, the **Quarterman** (GBR, 1226gt/73) was a product of Richard Dunston's shipyard at Hessle. She was launched on 18 January 1973 and delivered in June of that year to C Rowbotham & Sons (Management) Ltd. She had been designed to deliver refined products to Carrickfergus in Northern Ireland. In 1992, she was sold to operators in Tanzania and was renamed **DK II**. The photograph was taken at low water on 16 June 1984 and clearly shows the Wrach Channel marked off by buoys. Just visible to the right is Penarth pier, a popular calling point for Campbell steamers in years gone by and their present-day successors **Waverley** and **Balmoral**. The **Quarterman** is moored at a tidal oil berth which served a Texaco distribution depot. This berth fell into disuse after 1985 when new tax regulations relating to oil storage came into force. Many such sea-served terminals were closed, resulting in a considerable increase in road transport of refined products.

(Bernard McCall)

We now make our way in to Queen Alexandra Dock and we use photographs of three classic Dutch coasters to illustrate this. In the lock and awaiting departure in March 1968 is the **Makkum** (NLD, 381grt/52). Named after the location of the Amels shipyard where she was built, she was ordered as **Noord-West** but entered the water as **Makkum** on 25 June 1952. She was delivered to her Groningen-based owner on 30 September and was commercially managed by the huge Wagenborg company. In March 1963 she went to the Niestern shipyard where she was lengthened by 4,57 metres. Her first sale saw her bought by an owner in Panama in August 1972. She was renamed **Zubenelgenubi** and became **Samoa** two years later. Unusually, the next sale brought her back to Europe. She was acquired by owners in Malaga and renamed **Perez Munoz Primero** under the Spanish flag. Five years later she moved to Moroccan ownership and was renamed **Mazouja**. She was removed from Lloyd's Register in 2001 and her ultimate fate is unknown. The Queen Alexandra Dock was the last dock to be built in Cardiff. Its foundation stone is dated 22 October 1901 and it was opened by King Edward VII and Queen Alexandra in July 1907. Their royal yacht **Victoria and Albert** cut a ceremonial ribbon on entering the dock.

(John Wiltshire)

On 9 December 1971, the **Navigare** (NLD, 499grt/57) has just left the lock and starts to move into Queen Alexandra Dock. The coaster was built at the Jac. Bodewes shipyard in Bergum, now part of the Damen group. She was launched on 30 March 1957 and delivered to owner Willem Bootsman of Delfzijl as **Tubo** on 14 June. In August 1961 she was renamed **Moerdijk** for the duration of a time charter to Solleveld and Van der Meer, of Rotterdam, reverting to **Tubo** in June 1962. She became **Navigare** in 1970 and disappeared from movement lists when trading in the Caribbean in 1980 but is reported to have become **Paramount C** in 1982. Renamed **Eagle I** in 1986, there is much doubt about her later history but a reliable Dutch source suggests that she was renamed **Navigare** in 1991 and **Paramount C** once more in 1993. She was eventually removed from *Lloyd's Register* in 2009.

(John Wiltshire)

The management of the **Falcon** (NLD, 353grt/47) was the responsibility of a further large company based in the north of the Netherlands, namely Gruno. By coincidence, she had already been looked after by the other two companies. She was launched as **Rian** on 10 March 1947. Sadly she capsized on launching at the Bodewes shipyard in Martenshoek and one man was killed. She was raised ten days later and was eventually completed on 8 January 1948, entering trade within the Carebeka trading group. A sale within the Netherlands in April 1955 saw her renamed **Holwierde** with management transferring to Wijnne & Barends. Gruno took over when she became **Falcon** in January 1964. Sold without change of name to an owner in Guyana in October 1972, her career ended as it had begun. On 4 May 1973, she capsized at the quay at Port of Spain and was raised on 3 October. In 1975, she was reported to have been sold to buyers in Guyana and converted to a lighter. Of special interest in this view is the construction of the transit sheds on the north side of the dock. These have been used to store huge quantities of steel prior to export.

(John Wiltshire)

At the eastern end of Queen Alexandra Dock is Kings Wharf where a huge cold store was used for handling refrigerated cargoes. When the wharf was not being used by reefer vessels, it was often used as a lay-by berth. Noted there on 31 August 1968 was the **Martha Peters** (DEU, 1600grt/56). She was built by H C Stülcken Sohn at Steinwerder, Hamburg, where she was launched on 24 January 1956. She was handed over to Hamburg owners as **Tetuan** in April 1956. She was sold to other Hamburg owners and renamed **Martha Peters** in 1963. Acquired by Greek interests in 1978, she was renamed **Olympios Zeus**, later becoming **Georgios G** in 1980 and **Chrisanthi K** in 1984. She was laid up in September 1984 and was sold at auction in late 1985. Now hopelessly outdated, she was sold for scrap and arrived at Bombay (Mumbai) in March 1986.

(John Wiltshire)

Vessels sailing between Queen Alexandra Dock and Roath Dock navigate through a communication passage. Empire Wharf is located adjacent to this passage. Varied cargoes have been handled at this wharf including coal and general cargo. It is currently used for the discharge of sea-dredged aggregates. Such a use could not have been imagined when the **Trojan Prince** (GBR, 1283grt/54) was photographed there in August 1968. She was built at Bristol by Charles Hill & Sons Ltd and was launched on 18 November 1953. She was delivered to Coast Lines as **Lancashire Coast** in April 1954. She was chartered by Prince Line and renamed **Trojan Prince** in 1968 and reverted to her original name when the charter ended the following year. Soon afterwards, all her gear was removed and she was fitted to carry containers. In 1980 she was sold to Greek owners and, renamed **Paolino** and converted to a livestock carrier, was sometimes seen at Waterford where she loaded for Libya. She was eventually demolished at Salamis in Spring 1984. The brick building in the background is the cold store served by Kings Wharf.

(Bob Allen)

When photographed at Empire Wharf on 6 September 1962, the **Cortia** (SWE, 499grt/62) was in her first year of service. She was launched on 4 January 1962 at the Lödöse Varf shipyard on the eastern bank of the Göta Alv north of Gothenburg and was delivered to Swedish owners in April of that year. In 1966 she came under Ellerman control and her name was easily amended to **Cortian**, reverting to **Cortia** in 1971. She became **Austerity** in 1974 but the most significant point of her career came in 1978 when she was bought by Italian owners, renamed **Bruno Alpina**, and like the vessel seen above converted to a livestock carrier. A sale within Italy saw her become **Siba Foggia** in 1985 and she left European ownership eleven years later when renamed **Nehmet Allah** by Syrian operators. Later changes of identity saw her become **Fighter II** in 1977 and **Madar 1** in 1999. She is reported to have been scrapped but no precise details are known.

(John Wiltshire)

We continue through the communication passage and into Roath Dock completed in 1887. Dominating the background is the East Moors steelworks, built for the Dowlais Iron Company and opened on 4 February 1891. Various mergers, including one with Guest, Keen and Nettlefolds (better known as GKN), saw rapid growth which continued even during the recession of the 1930s. The decline of heavy industry in Wales during the mid-20th century resulted in the closure of East Moors in 1978. The *Hangudd* (FIN, 1110gt/58) was launched at the Van der Werf shipyard in Deest on 26 July 1958 and handed over as *Strib* to her Danish owners on 17 September. She was the third of three sisterships intended for transatlantic trade but was too small. With a crew of 18 but cargo capacity of only 1300 tonnes, the ships were clearly uneconomic. Her owners being in financial difficulties, she arrived at Copenhagen from Montreal on 26 June 1967 and was laid up without crew or heating during the autumn and winter months, inevitably suffering vandalism and damage. On 15 February, however, she was sold to Finnish owners and renamed *Hangudd* as seen here in March 1971. Sold to Irish owners and renamed *Ocean Trader* under the Panamanian flag in 1973, she became the Cypriot *Paravolas III* the following year. On 2 October 1979, she sank in the western Mediterranean soon after leaving Oran at the start of a voyage to Sharpness.

(Bob Allen)

The kangaroo cranes which used to discharge iron ore from ships for delivery to the adjacent East Moors steel works form an unusual backdrop for the *Con-Zelo* (GBR, 399grt/57) on 5 October 1969. The kangaroo crane was designed by Stothert & Pitt, renowned manufacturers of cranes. Instead of rotating the crane to deposit its load in a hopper on shore, a kangaroo crane has its own hopper beneath the jib. The coaster was launched at the Kramer & Booy shipyard in Spaarndam on 23 March 1957 and delivered to the van der Laan brothers, of Groningen, in July of that year. In 1961, she came into British ownership when bought by Jeppesen Heaton Ltd. For many years she imported timber from northern French ports to the Thames and Shoreham. This timber was used in the manufacture of furniture. She was sold to Italian owners and renamed *Femi* in 1990 but by April 1993 was reported to be laid up and under arrest at Lipari in Sicily. She was scrapped in 1997.

(John Wiltshire)

In the south-east corner of Roath Dock is an oil berth which has served various companies over the years including Gulf and latterly Texaco. Photographed discharging on 27 March 1970, the **Haförninn** (ISL, 2462gt/57), a name meaning "sea eagle", is a remarkable vessel. She was built at Haugesund and launched on 13 July 1957, being delivered as **Lønn** in November of that year to Norwegian tanker operator Odfjell. The turning point in her career came in 1966 when she was acquired by owners in Iceland and was converted to carry herring from fishing vessels to fish factories ashore. Her mainmast was removed and two goalpost masts added. All three masts were then fitted with the equipment clearly seen in this photograph. A movable lifting device was fitted to the rings atop each mast and this was used to steer the hoses used to pump the herring from the fishing vessels into the ship's tanks. In 1971 she was sold to Italian owners and renamed **Vallombrosa**. On 5 July 1986, she arrived at La Spezia to be repaired and subsequently moved on to Livorno, arriving on 19 November 1986 and remaining laid up there before eventually being scrapped at Olbia in early 1989.

(John Wiltshire)

We now move to the Roath Basin, constructed in 1874. The magnificent Pierhead Building dominates the background. This Grade 1 listed building was opened in 1897 and was the headquarters of the Bute Dock Company. In 1947, it became the administrative headquarters of the Port of Cardiff. In May 2001 it became a visitor and education centre for the Welsh National Assembly and nine years later was reopened as a Welsh history museum and exhibition. The **Sand Tern** (GBR, 535grt/64), photographed on 3 March 1991, had an unfortunate start to her career. She was launched at the Appledore shipyard of P K Harris on 22 May 1963 but this yard found itself in financial difficulties before the ship was completed so she was taken to Poole to be finished by J Bolson in April of the following year. In the late 1960s, she was used to carry construction materials to the site of the power station being built at Fawley. Mergers and takeovers within the dredging industry saw her change hands several times until she came into the ownership of British Dredging Aggregates in 1990. In the mid-1990s she was laid up at Barry and, having suffered suffered some vandalism, was eventually towed away and arrived at Bruges for demolition on 2 December 1998.

(Bernard McCall)

The name Associated Humber Lines had been used since 1935 to co-ordinate the Humber-based activities of five shipping companies and did not become a shipowner in its own right until 1957/58. It was owned by the British Transport Commission (91%) and Ellerman's Wilson Line (9%) and it inherited an obsolescent fleet from the BTC. It began a modernisation programme and built nine new vessels, the last of which was the **Selby** (GBR, 963grt/59). She was launched at the Port Glasgow shipyard of James Lamont & Co on 21 April 1959 and was delivered in June of that year. Intended for trade from the Ouse and Humber, she was transferred away to other routes in 1965. Photographed in the Roath Basin on 24 September 1968, she was no doubt awaiting her turn in drydock. Despite being outdated, she remained part of the British Rail fleet until 1974 when she was acquired by Pounds Marine. Sold on almost immediately to Greek owners, she was renamed **Raven**, becoming **Jean R** in 1977, **Victory** in 1980 and **Agios Nikolaos** in 1982. She was deleted from the Greek register in February 1988 after being declared a total loss but there are no details of the incident.

(John Wiltshire)

As Cardiff's docks grew ever larger during the latter half of the nineteenth century, so there was an increasing demand for ship repair facilities. Between 1850 and 1880, several companies established such facilities either along the River Taff or within the docks. By the 1970s, six drydocks remained. The three Mountstuart drydocks were outside the dock system and closed during that decade. The three that remained witnessed a steady decline in work and would eventually close for repair work by the end of the century as redevelopment spread through the docks area and notably the Roath Basin. Access to two of the three was gained through the Basin; the Channel Drydock was accessed directly from sea and was the first of these three to close.

The **Christian** (JAP, 1098grt/80) arrives in Bute Drydock from Dublin on 4 January 1983. She was one of four coastal tankers built in Japan between 1979 and 1981 and delivered for trade in northern Europe. She was launched on 16 June 1980 at the shipyard of Fukuoka Zosen K. K. and was delivered in October of that year. Management initially was the responsibility of Hull Gates Shipping Management Ltd, this transferring to Rowbotham Tankships Ltd in 1982. In August 1988, the tanker was acquired by F T Everard Shipping Ltd and renamed **Amity** under the Bahamas flag. In 2000, she was sold to Swedish owners and renamed **Smaragd**. A sale to Italian owners in Trieste in April 2009 saw her become a bunkering tanker named **Marisa N**.

(Bernard McCall)

All of the ports in South Wales require constant dredging in order to maintain an adequate depth of water in the fairways and within the enclosed docks. The bucket dredger **Abertawe** (GBR, 653grt/47) is an example of an older type of vessel long since replaced by suction dredgers. She was launched at the Paisley shipyard of Fleming & Ferguson on 5 June 1947 and delivered to her original owners, the Great Western Railway, in November of that year. She was eventually sold to owners in Naples and renamed **Santa Teresa** in 1972 and was removed from *Lloyd's Register* in 1987 when her continued existence was deemed to be in doubt.

(Nigel Jones)

Also seen in Commercial Drydock, the **Northlander** (USA, 300grt/77) is an intriguing vessel. She was the final vessel in a series of sixty-one built at the Nordsøværftet shipyard in Ringkøbing. The first in the series had been delivered in 1966 and this coaster was delivered under her original name of **Karl Frem** on 20 December 1977, having been launched on 18 November. She was sold and renamed **Niagara** in 1982 but five years later was bought by an American company based in Miami which had a time charter to the American army for transporting explosives from Nordenham to bases throughout northern Europe. She went to the Dannebrog shipyard in Århus where she was converted to a dedicated ammunition carrier with smoke detectors and sprinklers in the cargo hold. She often delivered ammunition to Barry and Newport and it was no surprise to see her in the Commercial Drydock in Cardiff in August 1988. After the charter expired in 1991, the **Northlander**, along with sistership **Oceanic** which had also been converted, was laid up at Nordenham. Sold back to Denmark, she was renamed **Sara Boye** in 1992 but two years later both were sold to a company in French Polynesia. The **Sara Boye** was renamed **Auura Nui III** and was converted yet again, this time allowing her to take passengers in addition to cargo. In 2000 she was renamed **Kura Ora III**.

(Bernard McCall)

The ports of Swansea, Port Talbot, Barry, Cardiff and Newport are all in the Associated British Ports Group and we now approach the last of those. Photographed off Newport on 29 August 1984, the **New Luck** (PAN, 366grt/45) has a long history. She was built for the Ministry of War Transport and was launched as **Empire Tapley** at the Northwich yard of Isaac Pimblott & Sons on 14 August 1944. She was renamed **Haifa** after sale to Danish owners on 19 October 1946 and then **Nord** following purchase by Swedish operators in January 1957. She was lengthened by 30 feet (9 metres) and three years later returned to Danish ownership as **Søren Rask**. In 1964 her original Polar engine of 460bhp was replaced by an Alpha of similar power. She left northern Europe in 1973 after acquisition by Greek owners who renamed her **Doryforos** (also noted as **Doriforos**). As such she arrived in the Bristol Channel in the late 1970s and was adapted to carry effluent from Newport to dumping grounds in the Channel. A reported name change to **Cyprus Star** in 1980 seems to have been erroneous but in 1981 she became **New Luck** under the flag of Panama. She was scrapped at Barry in December 1984.

(Danny Lynch)

The **Moldavia** (ATG, 1546gt/85) is also seen off Newport, the date being 16 July 2000. She was built at the Hugo Peters shipyard in Wewelsfleth and launched as **Dania Carina** on 9 March 1985. She was sold and renamed **Moldavia** in 1996 and joined the RMS fleet as **RMS Wedau** in 2003. Close inspection of the photograph will reveal a towline at the coaster's bow.

(Danny Lynch)

The reason for the towline was that the **Moldavia** was suffering engine problems and was being towed to Brunsbüttel by the tug **Vanguard**. The pair put into Mount's Bay on 17 July before continuing their voyage, arriving at Brunsbüttel on 21 July. Her departure was captured by two photographers and here we see her in the lock with the tug **I. B. Smith** providing assistance at her stern. The above photograph was, in fact, taken by the master of this tug. This lock was opened by Prince Arthur of Connaught on 14 July 1914. On this date, South Dock was fully opened. Some 48 acres had been opened seven years previously and was accessed via the East Lock which had been opened along with the first section of South Dock in 1893.

(Cedric Catt)

Approaching Newport at the end of a voyage from Santander on 2 April 1998, the **Lady Sylvia** (BHS, 1599gt/79) sports the colours of Rochester-based Thomas Watson (Shipping) Ltd. She was launched at the Bodewes Gruno shipyard in Foxhol on 21 September 1979 and delivered to Dutch owners as **Capricorn** on 8 October. She entered the Arklow Shipping fleet in 1985 and was renamed **Arklow Vale**, becoming **Inishfree** three years later following transfer within that fleet. She experienced a couple of problems subsequently. On Christmas Day 1990, she suffered main engine damage on passage from Limerick to Rochefort and had to be towed to Brest. She left on 3 January 1991 after repairs. Nineteen days later she grounded in the River Great Ouse at the start of a voyage from King's Lynn to Pasajes with wheat. She was refloated with tug assistance but inspections showed no apparent damage. She entered the Thomas Watson fleet as **Lady Sylvia** in summer 1994. Again she suffered a problem. On 23 November 1998 when heading for Belfast with wheat again from King's Lynn, she had to be towed into Swansea by fleetmate **Lady Sophia** (see page 92) because of severe vibration. She resumed her voyage on 8 January after crankshaft repairs. She was bought by Latvian owners in summer 1999 and was renamed **Elvita**, becoming **Elvita I** in 2007. She was to be renamed **Fotini** when acquired by Turkish owners in early 2010 but she seemingly never carried this name, instead becoming **Gulf Lion** a few months later.

(Danny Lynch)

We now move into the dock system at Newport. Many of the vessels featured in this book have a fascinating history and the **City** (GBR, 352grt/45) is no exception. She was built by W J Yarwood & Sons Ltd on the River Weaver at Northwich. She was completed for the Admiralty as coaling lighter **C633** in August 1945. She was one of five similar vessels bought by F T Everard in May 1956. After a period of lay up, the other four were taken to Goole and converted to tankers but this example, now renamed **City**, traded as a dry cargo ship until 1960 when she too was converted to a tanker. She spent most of her time on bareboat charter to Shell Mex & BP Ltd whose funnel colours she wears in this photograph taken when she was berthed at the oil depot at the eastern end of South Dock on 12 April 1969. She was then at the end of her career, being sold for demolition at Newport in July 1969.

(John Wiltshire)

The **Jul** (RUS, 2478gt/71) waits to discharge a cargo of timber from Riga at Newport's Middle Quay on 11 May 2003. This quay is on the eastern side of an extension of South Dock and was opened in 1893. For many years this quay was used to handle imports of fresh produce especially from Jamaica. The ship is one of a large class of sea/river ships built in Russia in the late 1960s and early 1970s. Known as the Sormovskiy class, most examples bore the name "Sormovskiy" followed by a serial number. Some, however, were given names that had a connection with Soviet or general communist history. Until 2000 this vessel was named **Parizhskaya Kommuna**, recalling the Paris Commune of 28 March to 28 May 1871, and no doubt named thus because her year of build marked the centenary of that first ever workers' government, albeit shortlived. In recent years, the ship has traded mainly in the Black Sea.

(Cedric Catt)

When Newport's North Dock was opened in 1875, it offered a huge improvement in accommodation at the port. The dock covered some 30 acres compared to the 12 acres previously available at Town Dock. With the transporter bridge (see page 82) clearly visible in the background, the **Merc Texco** (DNK, 399grt/69) was in excellent external condition when photographed in North Dock on 19 April 1972. Indeed she may have just emerged from the nearby drydock. Built by Frederikshavn Værft & Tordok, she was launched on 16 April 1969 and delivered to Per Henriksen on 3 June. She was the second in a series of six sisterships built at the yard for the Copenhagen-based owner. In 1975, she was sold to Indonesian owners and renamed **Darpo Delapan**, becoming **Manjjur** in 1994 and **Mercs Bolgoda** in 2000. She arrived at Mumbai for demolition on 26 April 2005.

(John Wiltshire)

The **Colston** (GBR, 586grt/55) has proved to be a remarkable survivor. She was built by Charles Hill & Sons at Bristol and was launched on 28 October 1954. On 6 January 1955 she was handed over to Bristol owners Osborn & Wallis for service in the company's coal trade between South Wales and Portishead. In the 1960s, she also loaded coal for the power stations at Yelland, near Barnstaple, and Hayle in Cornwall. She was sold in August 1970 to W E Dowds Ltd, a family company established in Newport in 1960. Between 1980 and 1987, she passed through the hands of various owning companies and had a period of lay up at Rochester in 1985/86. In late 1987,

she was sold to owners in the Caribbean where she has remained at work. Her solitary change of identity came in 1993 when renamed **Stengard** and she has been fitted with a deck-mounted crane amidships. In this view, taken on 9 November 1979, she is lying in Newport's North Dock, again seemingly having just emerged from the adjacent drydock. By a strange coincidence, the transit sheds on the quayside were taken over by W E Dowds Ltd when the company transferred its base from the River Usk to the enclosed docks (see page 84).

(Danny Lynch)

All too soon we are leaving Newport docks with the **Eden Fisher** (GBR, 1173grt/65) approaching the lock at the western end of South Dock on 14 April 1971. The ship was built at Foxhol for James Fisher & Sons Ltd, of Barrow. She remained in British ownership when sold in 1979, the buyers being Liverpool-based S William Coe by whom she was renamed **Blackthorn**. Even when sold to Bahamas-flag operators in 1985, she continued to trade in familiar waters in northern Europe. On 14 September 1989, when on passage from Pasajes to Sharpness, her cargo shifted and she started to list. She was towed to Brest after being abandoned by her crew. Early the following year, she was sold to Greek owners and was renamed **Poseidon**. She continued to call at UK ports, often loading clay at Bideford or Teignmouth for the Mediterranean. Further sales within Greece saw her become **Armenistis** in 1993 and **Georgia M** in 2004. She is believed to be still in service.

(John Wiltshire)

Danish shipowners have always displayed immense pride in their vessels and have taken every opportunity to display their nationality. A stern view of the *Dansus* (DNK, 1042gt/85) as she entered the River Usk immediately after leaving the lock rather than this image of her in the lock would have shown that her owner had used the Danish flag as the basis of his funnel design. She was built at the Nordsøværftet shipyard in Ringkøbing and, having been launched on 16 November 1984, was delivered to Marstal-based owner Peter Jørs on 17 January 1985. She was sold in June 2005 and was renamed *Mirella* under the Panamanian flag. Two years later, she was bought by Indian owners and became *ITT Panther*. Flying the flag of India, she maintains a service between Kolkata (Calcutta) and Port Blair, the capital of the Andaman and Nicobar Islands in the Indian Ocean. This photograph shows her at the start of a voyage to Amsterdam on 12 May 1999.

(Danny Lynch)

Our survey of coastal vessels in South Wales is far from over because we now turn eastwards to the River Usk. Passing the appropriately named Uskmouth B power station on 5 August 2002 is the **Fast Wil** (NLD, 1391gt/85). Fast Lines was established in the 1980s by Herman Scheers who was handling exports of chemicals from Szczecin to UK ports. The company expanded rapidly through the 1990s and acquired its own coasters in addition to taking some on charter. At the time of writing in mid-2011, it remains in the ownership of the Scheers family. It owns five vessels, one of these being the

Fast Wil. She was heading for Lysaghts Wharf where she loaded steel for Bilbao. The ship was built at the Bijlsma shipyard in Wartena in the north of the Netherlands. She was named **Christina** until acquired by Fast Lines in 1997 during the company's period of expansion, the renaming taking place in mid-November. The nearby Uskmouth A power station was demolished in 2002 and a new combined cycle gas turbine power station has been built on the site.

(Bernard McCall)

The **Rana** (NLD, 1780gt/00) rounds Powderhouse Point almost at the end of a voyage from Pasajes on 26 August 2002. To keep costs down, many European shipbuilders have built the hulls of new vessels at associated shipyards in eastern Europe and the **Rana** is a good example. Her hull was built by Rechytskiy Sudostroitelnyy Zavod at Rechytsa, a town in Belarus. This hull was then towed to the Damen shipyard in Bergum for completion and the completed vessel, an example of the Damen Combi Coaster 2500 design, was handed over to Harlingen-based owners in April 2000. In 2005, she was sold within the Netherlands and renamed **Rhoon**. Five years later she was bought by Cebo Marine and renamed **Rhoon-C**. Dominating the background is Uskmouth B power station, built in 1959. It closed in 1995 but was reopened in 2001 after a 3-year refurbishment programme costing over £100 million. Sadly it was forced to close after only one year when the owners went into receivership. It returned to full operation in June 2004 after being bought by Welsh Power and five years later it was sold to Scottish & Southern Energy plc. Although situated by the river, it has never been provided with a wharf and its deliveries of coal are brought by rail.

(Bernard McCall)

With the transporter bridge (see pages 82 and 83) unable to cope with ever-inceasing traffic, a new bridge over the Usk was opened in 1964. It was named rather prosaically George Street Bridge and it was from that bridge that the **Glen Gower** (GBR, 552grt/63) was photographed on 11 June 1976. This sand dredger was launched at the Ferus Smit shipyard in Foxhol on 6 April 1963 and delivered in the following month to owners South Wales Sand & Gravel and was a sistership of the **Glen Hafod** delivered from the same yard in December 1960. The **Glen Gower** was eventually demolished at Bow Creek on the River Thames in the summer of 1993.

(Cedric Catt)

The **Portelet** (GBR, 1042grt/61) was built at the Gideon Koster shipyard in Groningen for Channel Islands operator Onesimus Dorey. She was launched in July 1961 and delivered in October of that year. She was sold to Lebanese owners in 1978 and after a short period laid up at St Sampsons, Guernsey, under her new name of **Abdullah**, she departed for the Mediterranean. Sold within Syria in 1981, she was renamed **Hikmat** and in 1995 was removed from *Lloyd's Register* as her existence was in doubt. Doubtful it may have been, but she was certainly very much intact and was photographed at the Syrian port of Tartous in late October 2000. There has been no further news of her since that time. The ship is passing beneath the transporter bridge, opened on 12 September 1906 after a construction period of four years. One of only two such structures remaining in the UK which are able to carry motorised traffic, pedestrians and up to six cars are carried across the river on a platform or gondola which is suspended from a traveller running along a track between two lattice towers.

(Cedric Catt)

The **City of Cardiff** (GBR, 2074gt/97) was launched by Appledore Shipbuilders in March 1997 and delivered to the United Marine Group three months later. In the mid-20th century, the Bristol Channel was the base for a large number of sand dredgers but company mergers and partnerships along with the increasing size of the latest generations of dredgers have resulted in just six vessels sharing the majority of the work on both sides of the Channel. Four of these are pairs of sisterships and we see one pair on this and the following page. Although the **City of Cardiff** is usually to be found in the Bristol Channel, she makes deliveries to several ports on the west coast of the UK as far north as Heysham. Having discharged at Great Western Wharf on the eastern bank of the Usk, she passes beneath the transporter bridge in July 2002. Although the bridge was given Grade II listed status in 1979, it had to be closed for safety reasons in the mid-1980s. A major renovation programme began in 1992 and the bridge was re-opened in December 1995, its status being upgraded to Grade I the following year.

(Bernard McCall)

When the **City of Cardiff** is not available, she is replaced by her sistership, the Littlehampton-registered **City of Chichester** (GBR, 2074gt/97) which is generally based on the south coast of England. The pair of dredgers, which replaced four smaller dredgers, was ordered by United Marine Dredging, part of the United Marine Holdings Group owned jointly by Tarmac Quarry Products Ltd and Pioneer Concrete Holdings Ltd. The **City of Chichester**, launched at the Appledore shipyard on 5 July 1997 and completed during October, is seen at Great Western Wharf on 22 February 1998. The wharf was built in 1875 and had its own private railway connecting with the Great Western Railway using its own two locomotives and approximately five hundred wagons. It boasted four steam cranes and a coal hoist and was ideally located to serve the collieries and iron works of Monmouthshire. The construction and opening in November 2004 of a new road bridge over the Usk rendered this wharf inaccessible and a large housing estate has been built on the site.

(Cedric Catt)

On page 76, we noted that W E Dowds Ltd had transferred its cargo handling from a private berth on the River Usk to the enclosed docks. At low water on 10 September 1987, we see the **Rolf D** (DEU, 996grt/70) at the private wharf known as Penmaen Wharf or, not surprisingly, simply Dowds Wharf. She had brought 1700 tonnes of rape seed extract meal from Rotterdam. The Hugo Peters shipyard in Wewelsfleth, although not as well known as the Sietas yard on the outskirts of Hamburg, nevertheless has played an important role in coaster construction. One of its most successful and aesthetically-leasing designs was that known as the Euro class dating from the late 1960s. The high cubic capacity and low gross tonnage made these vessels popular for the growing container trade and especially for the carriage of packaged timber.

The first eight ships were built for Hamburg owner Gunther Graebe. Construction of the hulls of four of these was subcontracted to Stader Schiffswerft which had closed in 1967. The second of these four was launched as **Heidberg** but entered service as **Skeppsbron** although she reverted to **Heidberg** in 1972. Sales and charters within Germany saw her become **Jenny Graebe** (1978), **Euro Sailer** (1983) and **Rolf D** (1987). Later sales saw her become **Fiina Timber** (1997), **Miina** (2000), **Maleka M** and **Omar J** (2005), and **Ibrahim M** (2006). Located on the western bank of the river just upstream from the transporter bridge, the wharf itself has been refurbished and is used for passengers sailing on Bristol Channel excursion vessels.

(Cedric Catt)

Staying on the western bank of the Usk, there is a series of wharves which saw sporadic commercial use during the last three decades of the twentieth century. The **Danica Green** (DIS, 902gt/81) swings in the River Usk and edges towards Commercial Wharf at the end of a voyage from Dordrecht on 11 July 1999. She was the first of ten similar vessels, all with the "Danica" prefix, built for Danish owner H Folmer by the Sakskøbing shipyard in Denmark. Her sistership is **Danica Red** and as the series expanded through the 1980s, the later vessels were slightly longer and in the early 1990s they were followed by three more vessels, this time having a "Danica" suffix. The company was founded in 1955 by Helge Folmer, a shipbroker based in Copenhagen, and remains a family-owned company. Its vessels maintain the Danish tradition of worldwide trading.

(Cedric Catt)

A panoramic view of this section of river on 26 May 1997. At Commercial Wharf is the **Arklow View** (IRL, 2827gt/91), the penultimate vessel in a series of eight built at the Hugo Peters shipyard. She was launched on 4 August 1991 and delivered to Arklow Shipping on 17 September. She had arrived from Bermeo the previous day and departed for El Ferrol on 30 May. She was sold to Norwegian owners in early 2006 and was renamed **Jomi** under the Bahamas flag during April. By coincidence, both vessels in this photograph were built at the Hugo Peters shipyard in Wewelsfleth situated on the River Stör, a tributary of the River Elbe. The **Sindbad** (CYP, 1499gt/81) had just arrived at Risca Wharf from Bremen and departed for Rouen three days later. In summer 2005, she was sold to owners in Montevideo and was renamed **Lucero** under the flag of Uruguay. She left Dordrecht on 25 August 2005 heading for Las Palmas and then across the Atlantic.

(Cedric Catt)

The **Sand Jade** (GBR, 398grt/54) heads up river and has just passed George Street bridge on the late afternoon tide of 11 June 1976. Visible in the distance are two minesweepers awaiting demolition at Cashmore's yard. They are the French minesweepers **Persée** and **Aldebaran** which had arrived on 1 April. Cashmore's aso scrapped a large number of locomotives in addition to ships. Owned at the time by Sand Supplies (Western) Ltd, the **Sand Jade** was launched as **Auriga** on 12 December 1953 at the Westerbroek shipyard of

G J van der Werff. A conventional Dutch coaster, she was delivered as **Auriga-G** to owners in Groningen on 2 March 1954. In July 1971, she was sold to Sand Supplies (Western) Ltd and, renamed **Sand Jade**, was converted to a suction dredger at Saul on the Gloucester Canal. She traded as such for ten years before being sold to owners in Hartlepool and renamed **Dianne K**. She left the UK in 1987 following purchase by owners in Malta and survived until 1996 when she arrived for demolition at Aliaga in Turkey.

(Cedric Catt)

Our photographer wisely followed the **Sand Jade** and **Glen Gower** to their berths on 11 June 1976. The latter vessel is discharging at the Blaenavon Wharf of British Dredging whilst the **Sand Jade** discharges at Newport Sand & Gravel's Moderator Wharf. After the demise of Newport Sand & Gravel, the wharf was taken over by Peter J Dallimore who had been a manager and weighbridgeman for the company and also a haulage contractor for them and for other sand importers. The wharf then became known as Dallimore's Wharf.

The story is continued on page 90. It is worth noting that in 1871 there were more than 60 wharves on the River Usk in the Newport area. By 1934, the number had fallen to 24. The construction of leisure facilities and new roads was responsible for the closure of several wharves in the 1990s. As this book is being written in mid-2011, there are only three wharves still handling commercial trade.

(Cedric Catt)

The story of Lysaght's steel works on the eastern bank of the Usk is a remarkable one. The company was established in Bristol in the latter half of the nineteenth century and made its fortune by the production of galvanised corrugated sheet in Bristol and Wolverhampton, using the name Orb. It opened its works in Newport in March 1898. The huge works has now been demolished and replaced by a housing estate but its private jetty has survived to serve what remains of the former Llanwern steelworks, now owned by Tata. Lysaght's Wharf, also known as Orb Jetty, is a good example of a NAABSA wharf, the letters standing for "Not Always Afloat But Safe Aground" and this photograph of the **RMS Auriga** (ATG, 2456gt/96) on 27 July 1997 offers a vivid image of such a wharf and of the nature of the bed of the River Usk at this point. She had arrived from Dundalk and sailed two days later to Antwerp with a cargo of steel. The ship is a further example of the "Rhein" class from the Slovenske Lodenice shipyard in Komarno, a town located at the junction of the Rivers Danube and Vah in Slovakia. She was launched as **Auriga** but delivered to her German owners as **RMS Auriga** for the duration of a charter to RMS. In 1999, she reverted to her original name but in March of the following year she became **Wani Auriga**, again for the duration of a charter. Becoming **Auriga** once again in mid-2001, she kept this name until 2007 when she was purchased by Norwegian owners, renamed **Hagland Bona**, and fitted with a Hitachi excavator for self discharge.

(Cedric Catt)

At some stage in the late 1990s or early 2000s, it was decided to improve the Uskside landscape opposite Lysaght's Wharf. Much debris was cleared away and an attractive area was created with information plaques about the history of the locality and about the birds that could be seen. Sadly this too has now been swept away in the wake of the construction of a new road and the area once again looks shabby and unwelcoming. This is especially regrettable as the site is that of a former lock at the entrance to the old dock system. The visitor area is prominent in this view of the **Arklow Bay** (IRL, 1524gt/88) loading steel at the wharf on 6 April 2001. The coaster was launched at the Hugo Peters shipyard in Wewelsfleth on 20 February 1988 and she was delivered on 20 March. Some sources claim that she was launched as **Arklow Mansion** but this is not correct although it is true to say that the name **Arklow Mansion** had been provisionally allocated when her keel was laid. She was sold to Norwegian owners and renamed **Frakt** in June 2004. Steel making ceased at Llanwern in 2001 and a large section of the works was demolished in 2004. The Indian steel maker Tata acquired a section of the works for hot and cold strip rolling and hot dip galvanising and has been using the wharf for imports. It was taken out of use, however, in 2010 although this was said to be only a temporary measure.

(Bernard McCall)

During the 1980s, the local council sought to take over the wharves near the town centre and Peter Dallimore (page 87) was offered a berth in Newport docks. This he declined because of the extra costs that would be incurred. Consequently the council then offered him facilities at a berth on the east side of the river and this became known as Dallimore's Wharf. The wharf is now owned by Hanson and the usual callers are the **Arco Dee** (GBR, 1309gt/90) and sistership **Arco Dart**. The **Arco Dee** was the second of the pair of dredgers built for ARC Marine by IHC Holland at Sliedrecht in the Netherlands. She is a self-discharging dredger designed to be able to discharge at a riverside wharf such as this one over the period of a single tide. The transporter bridge is clearly visible upstream in the distance and the overhead power lines come from Uskmouth power station.

(Bernard McCall)

Two drydocks were constructed on the eastern bank of the Usk in the late nineteenth century. Known as the Union Dry Docks, they were later used as commercial docks. The smaller one became known as Eastern Dry Dock and was used mainly for the export of woodchips and import of sand. The **Sheila Hammann** (DEU, 1022gt/83) was just making fast when photographed on 30 March 1990 and was about to load woodchips for Dordrecht. She was built by Kötter Werft at Haren/Ems and was delivered to Wischhafen-based owners Hammann & Prahm on 27 October 1983 after being launched earlier that month. On 8 December 1992, she was renamed **RMS Anglia** at Boston (Lincs) for the duration of a charter to RMS and reverted to **Sheila Hammann** at Nantes on 9 September 1996. She retained this name until sold to Uwe Werner and renamed **Karina W** at Bremen on 4 May 2006. Incidentally, personnel were transferred beween ship and shore using the grab of the crane. The berth is currently out of use because of siltation.

(Bernard McCall)

It was in 1964 that Bell Lines took over the other former drydock on the eastern bank of the River Usk and, having renamed it Bellport, continued to use it until 1993 when the company moved its Bristol Channel terminal to Avonmouth. The **Rosita Maria** (NIS, 999grt/77) was one of the final callers at Bellport and had arrived from Bilbao when photographed in late November 1993. Launched on 27 January 1977 and delivered to Lübeck-based owners on 3 March, she was the penultimate vessel in the Type 81 series from the J J Sietas shipyard near Hamburg, a series which totalled twenty-two ships. The Type 81 design was essentially a container feeder and many later designs were based on it but it could also serve as a useful general cargo vessel. She spent many years on Bell Lines routes before that company ceased trading in the mid-1990s. Sold in 2002, she was renamed **Rosita** and as such worked for a time between Aberdeen, Kirkwall and Lerwick on the Streamline service. After being laid up at Lübeck in late 2008, she was sold and renamed **Axiom II** in Autumn 2009. She arrived at Southampton on 26 October 2009 after breaking down in the English Channel and remained there until eventually leaving for Gijon and then the Mediterranean on 10 July 2010.

(Bernard McCall)

In 1993, Bell Lines decided to transfer its Bristol Channel terminal from Bellport to Avonmouth. The valuable asset was soon sold for general cargo handling and the unique Goliath crane, able to lift 43 tons, was retained. The dock is 225 metres long and 19,8 metres wide. Although able to accommodate vessels of up to 8000 tonnes deadweight, it has rarely done so but it often accommodates two smaller vessels simultaneously and at the time of writing is being extensively used by Tata. It has been renamed Birdport. Having suffered engine problems after arrival from Eregli, the **Lady Sophia** (BHS, 2208gt/77) is about to be towed to Newport docks for repair. She was eighteen years old when she came into the ownership of Thomas Watson (Shipping) Ltd. She was launched at the Hjørungvåg shipyard in Norway on 5 March 1977. Three months later she was delivered to Danish owners as **Atlantic Progress** but by the end of the year had been sold to Dutch owners and renamed **Holberg**. Sold within the Netherlands in 1979, she was then lengthened by 18,34 metres. She hoisted the Austrian flag as **Enns** in 1984 and eleven years later came into British ownership when bought by Thomas Watson (Shipping) Ltd and renamed **Lady Sophia**. Sold to Turkish owners in mid-July 1999, she became Costanza under the flag of Malta. Since then she has had other names, always remaining in Turkish ownership but using various flags and trading mainly in the Black Sea. These names have been **Goodness** (2002), **A Akdeniz** (2007) and **Nur** (2009).

(Danny Lynch)

We are almost back at Uskmouth and our final wharf is Alpha Steel Wharf. Alpha Steel was established in 1974 and originally produced steel slabs for its own hot strip mill. In 1988 it began to produce steel billets in order to widen its market. Taken over by Iranian owners in July 2003, there were promises of huge growth and investment but in December 2007 the company went into administration and the future looked very bleak. Thankfully a buyer was found in the form of a Russian company which established Mir Steel on the site and production resumed in July 2010. Because of the nature of Alpha Steel's products, most of the arrivals were much larger vessels taking export cargoes worldwide but mainly to the Mediterranean, the smallest noted for our purposes was the **Atlantic Mercado** (ATG, 3422gt/76) seen loading for Leixoes on 26 October 2000. The ship was built for Spliethoff's Bevrachtingskantoor, of Amsterdam, by Miho Zosensho K. K. at Shimizu in Japan. She was launched on 10 November 1976 and delivered as **Rijpgracht** on 17 December. Sold out of the Spliethoff fleet in 1989, she became **Eliza** and then in 1990 was bought by Cypriot-flag operators and renamed **Atlantic Mercado**. She was laid up after arrival at Durban on 4 August 2005 and was sold at public auction in early December of that year. Her new Syrian owners renamed her **Anastasia** and she became **Master Fawaz** in 2008.

(Cedric Catt)

We are coming to the end of our look at coastal vessels in South Wales and we look briefly at the River Wye which forms the border between England and Wales. The historic port of Chepstow is now used only for the import of sand dredged in the Bristol Channel. From 1995, the main vessel importing sand was the appropriately-named *Severn Sands* (GBR, 515gt/60) photographed in the River Wye on 10 April 2005. She was built by N. V. Scheeps "Westerbroek" and launched as *Isca* in mid-September 1960. She was the first vessel owned by Western Dredgers Ltd, based at Moderator Wharf on the River Usk. This company was acquired by the British Dredging group in 1966.

After being laid up at Cardiff in 1975, she was sold to owners in Brittany in 1976 and was renamed *Le Ferlas*, this being modified to *Ferlas* in 1989. Remarkably she returned to South Wales in early 1995 and was renamed *Severn Sands*. After a decade as such, she made her final commercial voyage with a cargo from the Bedwin Sands to Newport on 28 April 2005. Following a period laid up, she was sold and moved to the River Taw but plans to use her as a house boat came to nothing and after being driven upstream during a heavy storm she was abandoned by her owner and demolished at Yelland in 2010.

(Nigel Jones)

The **Severn Sands** was succeeded by the **Argabay** (GBR, 756gt/89). This vessel was built by the Yorkshire Dry Dock Co Ltd at Hull. She was launched on 3 June 1989 and delivered as **Hoo Maple** to Jacobs & Partners Ltd in September, being bareboat chartered to her managers R Lapthorn & Co Ltd. The **Hoo Maple** arrived at Newport on 6 April 2004 and underwent a conversion that lasted a year. Two new cargo holds were installed and she was fitted with a dredging pipe and pump. She entered service on 4 May 2005 and four days later made her first voyage to Chepstow. We see her inward bound during that initial voyage. After entry into service, she was fitted with a grab for self discharge. The grab is located centrally between the two holds and can discharge a full cargo of 900 tons of sand in three hours. This was the second time in her career that she had been equipped for self-discharge. As **Hoo Maple**, she was one of two Lapthorn coasters selected for adaptation to self-discharge and a Samsung excavator and grab was fitted amidships in 1995.

(Nigel Jones)

It would be difficult to compile a book such as this without including a vessel from the fleet of one of the last shipowners to be based in South Wales, namely Charles Willie (Shipping) Ltd. The shipping company was established in 1938 but its name had appeared on railway wagons as early as 1912 when it was noted as colliery agents, coal exporters and importers of pit props. Although trading throughout Europe, its core services have linked the UK to the Iberian peninsula. The **Biscay Pride** (BHS, 695grt/78) was undergoing routine maintenance when photographed in Cardiff's Bute Drydock on 23 December 1988. The coaster was launched at the Astilleros Luzuriaga shipyard in Pasajes on 18 October 1978 and delivered to Spanish owners as *Izarraitz* in December. She entered the Willie fleet in 1987 and remained until 8 May 1995 when she was renamed **Roin I** at Castellon. In 1997 she was sold and renamed **Estela**, becoming **Brigo** in mid-January 2000. She then disappeared from movement reports until arriving at Aviles for demolition on 5 October 2000.

(Bernard McCall)

Flag abbreviations

ATG	Antigua & Barbuda	JAP	Japan
BEL	Belgium	LBN	Lebanon
BHS	Bahamas	LBR	Liberia
CYP	Cyprus	LTU	Lithuania
DEU	Germany	MLT	Malta
DIS	Danish International	NLD	Netherlands
DNK	Denmark	NIS	Norwegian International
EST	Estonia	NOR	Norway
FIN	Finland	PAN	Panama
GBR	United Kingdom	RUS	Russia
GRC	Greece	SWE	Sweden
IOM	Isle of Man	USA	United States of America
IRL	Republic of Ireland	VUT	Vanuatu
ISL	Iceland		